TODDLER DISCIPLINE
FOR EVERY AGE AND STAGE

toddler discipline
for Every Age and Stage

Effective Strategies to Tame Tantrums,
Overcome Challenges, and Help Your Child Grow

Aubrey Hargis
Foreword by Breana Sylvester, PhD

**ROCKRIDGE
PRESS**

To H and J—the mischief-making
duo who will forever own my heart.

Designer: Christopher T. Fong
Editor: Katharine Moore
Production Editor: Erum Khan
Cover Photography © Maroke/iStock

ISBN: Print 978-1-64152-127-7 | eBook 978-1-64152-128-4

Contents

Foreword

As an educational psychologist who works with young children and the mother of a 5-year-old, supporting children's development and well-being is both my passion and my profession. *Toddler Discipline for Every Age and Stage* addresses so much of what I have learned and practiced over the years. It is a clear and organized guide that you'll take down from the shelf often as a reference and reminder, both when you are looking forward to the next milestone and when things aren't going according to plan.

One of my favorite things about this book is Aubrey's reminder that the first step in disciplining our children is to ask ourselves whether our child's action (e.g., eating with her fingers) is actually a problem. This book tells us to focus on priorities and on what *is* under our control (guidance I would do well to heed at the dinner table).

My son is a talker; he takes part in discussions of concepts beyond his years. Given his language skills, it has always been easy to assume that just because he can talk about what we're asking of him, he can *do* it; so when he struggles with coordination, it can lead to frustration for him and us. Aubrey's elegant presentation of what to expect from children at each stage, coupled with reminders that every child's development follows its own trajectory, helps us meet our children where they are. For now, I can rest easy knowing someday my kid will eat his noodles with utensils.

In reading this book, you will discover joy in connecting your child's needs, interests, and preferences to his behaviors and learn to look through the lens of his developmental tasks at each stage. You will gain insights into how to shape your home environment to best support your child's needs, explore ways to help your child manage her emotions, and learn strategies to say "Yes" as often as possible.

As Aubrey so keenly states, parenting is the ultimate opportunity to grow as a human being. I encourage you to embrace the guidance given in this book; it will support you in forming and maintaining a cooperative relationship with your child, and in having fun along the way!

—Breana Sylvester, PhD

Founder, Growing Curiosity Early Learning

Introduction

He glares at me from across the kitchen, eyes squinting in fury, face reddening as he holds his breath. Headfirst and full force, he runs toward my belly, and upon contact, mashes himself against me. His arms are flailing, and I can't tell if he's actively trying to hit me or if he's just out of control. My biceps are still stronger than his so I use them to hold him at bay without hurting him. He screeches in protest and reaches for my waist. I can see tears forming in the corners of his eyes. I feel awful inside.

In my head, I am running through all the discipline strategies I know and I'm second-guessing all of my decisions. Did I make the wrong choice by setting a limit? Was I too harsh or unsympathetic? Am I a pushover? And the worst thought of all—am I failing as a parent?

I give up fighting him. Heart pounding, I reverse the energy flow and hug him tightly instead. I yell, "You're mad at me! You're really, really mad! I'm sorry we're fighting. I don't want to fight. I love you. I love you so much!" His body goes rag-doll limp. He takes a shaky breath and lets out a sob. We melt to the floor together, a tangle of bent knees and bowed heads. I still don't know if the way I handled the situation would seem right or wrong in anyone else's eyes, but my own uniquely impulsive and intensely emotional child accepts the cuddle. I rock us back and forth for a long time, whispering, "I love you, I love you, I love you."

Every time we interact with our children, we have the opportunity to coach them on how to manage their own emotions and behave appropriately in social situations. It isn't easy; our own personalities and insecurities greatly influence how we address a challenging behavior in our children.

As the daughter of a Montessori preschool teacher and a psychologist, child development was a frequent dinner table topic. By the time I was 13, I was completely hooked. My childhood heroes were Alfie Kohn and Madelyn Swift, two fierce proponents of a more positive, compassionate approach to discipline. I also became aware that I was being raised differently from many of my peers: While my friends and cousins were spanked or grounded, I was counseled. But it wasn't exactly easy to come clean, reveal my emotions, and mutually agree upon solutions, so sometimes being punished seemed like the easy way out! Still, I grew up with a heavy appreciation of the time my parents spent with me to offer their guidance, and the fair and respectful treatment of children became the golden, wrapped-up package in my soul.

After several years of teaching kindergarteners and a whole lot more personal research on disciplinary techniques and strategies to handle defiance, effective parenting seemed so *easy.* When I saw a child having a tantrum in the grocery store, I assumed that if the parent had been proactive in the right way, the whole embarrassing conflict could have been avoided. In the words of Bob Dylan, "Ah, but I was so much older then. I'm younger than that, now."

The first time I had to handle a tantrum from my own child, I was knocked flat off my feet! All the strategies I had learned by heart now had to be implemented in practice, not just preached. The complete lack of objectivity had rendered me a newbie in the field. What I had learned to be true from the books now had to be learned all over again from experience. And so, my children set about teaching me the right way to parent them.

Now, as a parent coach and educational consultant, I listen to the concerns and anxieties of many parents in the thick of those tough toddler years, and my heart aches in remembrance. Parenting is a humbling experience. Children pass through such a quickly progressing succession of developmental stages during the first few years of life that it's hard for us to keep up with their current needs, much less anticipate what changes will occur next. As my mama always said with a bit of cheekiness, "If you don't like your child's behavior, just wait a few weeks for a new developmental stage. By then, you'll have an entirely different problem to figure out!"

In addition, most of us have no real memories of what it felt like to be a toddler. We can only imagine the intensity of their emotions as they push toward independence and simultaneously demand the safety and comfort that can only be provided by a parent.

You, like your child, are on a path of *becoming*. Your quest: to nurture your child's potential, and while doing so, learn how to become a stronger and more compassionate human being yourself. Every day, you bravely face the possibility of tantrums and acts of defiance, obstacles that would ruffle even the most heroic among us. Yet you are never alone in these woods.

Unlike in a fairy tale, there is no magic wand or spell that can skip you to the happily-ever-after; however, what I can offer you is a map that reveals your child's natural developmental path. I can also help fill the backpack for this journey with discipline strategies to pick and choose from as you learn what works best for you and your child. I can give you a heads-up about the issues parents commonly face during each year so that you know what to look for. And I can reassure you that there is no such thing as perfection. We all make mistakes and learn from them. Our children's capacity for forgiveness and acceptance of our faults is unfathomable. As long as you are meeting your child's basic needs for health, safety, and love, you will walk right out of these dark woods into the sunlight. I promise.

CHAPTER
ONE

Discipline and Your Toddler

No doubt, you would like to have a well-behaved child. You may even be feeling pressure from family members, friends, and strangers you meet on the street to make sure your mini-me stays polite and quiet. Here's the good news: You can have a well-behaved child. The bad news: You can't have one all of the time. By the very nature of human brain development, our children require time, patience, and guidance to learn how to treat others with respect and regulate their own emotional states.

What Is Discipline?

How do you make a child behave? The answer may be shocking: you don't. He alone is able to choose to modify his behavior within the scope of his current developmental capabilities. But you have a lot of power as his parent. You can help him make the choice to comply or cooperate with your requests, and you can teach him about the behavioral expectations for different situations in your culture. He needs *discipline*. To use the transitive verb to bring home the point, he needs *to be disciplined* by you.

Parenting experts still debate about what effective discipline for young children looks like, and there are many techniques you can try. Punishment may immediately come to mind, but routine spanking or smacking, isolating, or taking away possessions, privileges, or experiences from a child can have unintended consequences later on in life. When you use punishment as a discipline technique, you are sending your child the message that you want him to suffer for his actions. In his subconscious, he is making the connection that your love is equal to your approval.

As the parent enforcing a rule with punishment, you may see yourself as "taking charge" or "laying down the law." What you might not see is that underneath his compliance, he is choosing to change his behavior because he afraid of being hurt or abandoned. Many adults who were punished severely as children struggle with higher levels of stress that can lead to excessive guilt, anxiety, or depression. Others struggle to maintain healthy, trusting relationships with others. In contrast, the reasonable use of consequences, which may involve removing your child from an unsafe or problematic situation, does not have the same impact. Setting limits on unsafe or inappropriate behavior leads to positive results. See page 91 for a fuller explanation of consequences and how to use them in a nonpunitive way.

Quick Tip: It can be emotionally difficult for us to disagree with the way our own parents raised us. Rejecting the use of a discipline technique does not devalue the worth of a relationship or negate the positive contributions of a person. Since your parenting journey involves a good bit of self-reflection, I invite you to acknowledge any uncomfortable feelings and keep an open mind as you read the suggestions provided here.

When looking for positive alternatives to punishment, parents often turn to using rewards and praise to encourage respectful behavior. Proponents of this technique suggest handing out stickers, candy, and other special treats in exchange for compliance. Evaluative praise such as "I like the way you're sitting" or "Terrific job!" does provide positive reinforcement, but if praise is overused, the technique becomes emotionally manipulative. When the bribe or promise of your approval is no longer enticing enough to counter the potential thrill of breaking a rule, your children may one day intentionally choose not to receive it. This doesn't seem like a big deal when the disobedience is minor, such as when an older child refuses to turn off the TV at bedtime. It becomes a really big deal when the rule-breaking is harmful to oneself, others, or the environment, like drunk driving.

A better approach to disciplining your child is to use techniques that foster his ability to make moral judgments about right and wrong for himself. This does not mean letting him do whatever he wants. While he is a toddler, you are the one responsible for making any major decisions that you feel are in his best interest.

Since a toddler lacks the cognitive ability to use reason or logic to solve problems or decide what behavior is appropriate in any given situation, you will be coaching him step-by-step. His budding independence will emerge by making simple, meaningful choices at first. When he releases his big emotions and loses control, you will offer your support by empathizing and giving him the boundaries he needs in order to feel safe and loved.

Setting Realistic Goals

Parents often have expectations for behavior that aren't realistic given the ages of their children. To help you put things into perspective, each chapter of this book contains developmental information with suggestions for realistic behavioral expectations for each age and stage. This will help you know whether the technique you are choosing will support your short- or long-term goals for your child's growth and development.

Short-Term Goals

There will be times when you need to set a limit and either commit to enforcing it quickly or let go of your ideal routine. Here are few examples of some common short-term goals related to behavioral issues.

- Compliance for the sake of safety: see page 26, Distract and Redirect
- Getting a good night's sleep: see page 33, Bedtime Struggles
- Using good manners: see page 107, Going Out in Public
- Stopping the whining: see page 141, Putting an End to the Whining

Long-Term Goals

Recently, when I asked a group of parents to name the characteristics they hoped their children would embody someday in the future, nobody mentioned blind obedience. Instead, I received an inspiring list of lofty, optimistic long-term goals. These parents hoped their children would become adults who were happy, responsible, independent, compassionate, honest, determined, curious, resilient, intrinsically motivated, and good problem-solvers.

Take a few minutes to make a list of your own. You might start by thinking about what you consider to be your own strengths and the experiences that helped you develop them. Also think about your family and community values. Which would you consider a high priority?

As you pick and choose from among the discipline techniques proposed in this book, think about whether they support the long-term goals you have identified as being important for your child's future. For example, when you offer your 2-year-old a simple choice, like wearing a red shirt or a blue shirt, this is a small, supportive act of discipline that not only helps you avoid a morning meltdown, but also cultivates independence and responsibility. When you sit down with your 4-year-old and have a heart-to-heart conversation about why excluding another person from a group activity is hurtful, you are teaching him about compassion.

Disciplining your often unreasonable, highly emotional toddler can be frustrating. To remind yourself of these long-term goals, you might even keep this list in a place where you will see it daily, such as on the refrigerator, in your purse, or by the front door.

Temperament and Behavior

Your parenting style will have a significant influence on how your child behaves and perceives her place in the world, but it is not the only factor by far. Many people assume that a child's personality is always the direct result of how permissive or dictatorial the parent is. This is a myth. Your child is a unique and valuable person, born with a predisposition toward certain traits that developed in utero and continued to be formed by her experiences throughout early childhood.

In a revolutionary 1970 study of infant reactions to stimuli, Alexander Thomas, Stella Chess, and Herbert G. Birch determined that a child's "personality is formed by the constant interplay of temperament and environment." The nine temperament traits identified in this study give us insight into why children raised in similar environments may behave differently from one another.

Activity level: This trait refers to your child's general energy level. A high-energy child can be a handful with all the squirming and wiggling, while a more sedentary child can be hard to motivate physically, as quiet, calm activities are preferred. If your toddler is constantly climbing the furniture, running in circles, and popping in and out of bed at night, provide ample access to the outdoors on a daily basis so that her muscles have the freedom to move. Indoors, focus on ways to safely meet her need to stretch and explore independently.

Rhythmicity: How predictable is your child's natural, biological rhythm? Some children will eat, sleep, and have bowel movements with extreme regularity. For them, a predictable schedule is a comfortable one and largely self-determined. Other children show much more irregularity, which can complicate meals, naps, and toilet learning. Parental intervention and flexibility are necessary to avoid conflict.

Distractibility: Is your child easily distracted by outside influences? A child with high distractibility will often be satisfied when you exchange an unsafe object for a safe toy or when you sing a song while performing an unappealing task, such as buckling a car seat or changing a diaper. A child who is less willing to be distracted will not stop fussing until the task has been completed.

Initial response: When confronted with a new situation, such as a new person, food, toy, or activity, how eagerly does your child embrace the new experience? Some children approach them with ease, immediately interacting and engaging impulsively. Others are slow to warm up, taking time to get comfortable and assess the situation. When you introduce your child to a new person, such as a babysitter, she may prefer to sit quietly in your lap observing for a while before interacting. However, the withdrawal of some children from new experiences is much more dramatic and requires considerable adult encouragement and patience. A child with a negative initial response to new situations will cry, hide, or run away. She will need emotional support and lots of time to adjust to new experiences.

Adaptability: This refers to your child's ability to adjust over time to new experiences, routines, or expectations. If your child is adaptable in temperament, transitioning from one activity to another will not be a big deal. Settling into a new schedule may take some time, but you will not typically encounter much resistance from your child. Other children will react adversely to new routines, as evidenced by tantrums, defiance, or anxious behaviors. These children will benefit from more gradual shifts in routine rather than dramatic ones.

Attention span and persistence: Does your child concentrate on a single activity for a long time? Does she continue to repeat and practice new skills despite any obstacles in her way? The child with higher levels of attention and persistence will not give up easily when asked to perform tasks that are initially frustrating. On the other hand, if you interrupt this same child to ask her to move on to another activity, you may be met with resistance and an inflexible attitude. If your child has a shorter attention span and less persistence, she may need a more step-by-step approach, reminders, and visual cues to help her complete difficult tasks.

Intensity of reaction: How strongly does your child show her emotions? Very intense children may be labeled as "overdramatic," celebrating with extreme exuberance when excited and sobbing or tantruming over minor disappointments. Children with lower levels of intensity may smile or cry, but in general their reaction to events will be much more subdued by comparison.

Parent to Parent:
Loving Those Personality Differences

"My 3-year-old is very sensitive. He needs time to adjust to new situations and warm up to people, although he craves physical affection with us. He is also very caring, independent, logical, and clever. He is an outside-of-the-box thinker. I definitely need to empathize with him a lot and give him the space and time he needs to get used to a new place or new people. Everyone calls him shy, but he is just cautious. He also gets very frustrated pretty easily. He needs someone to be gentle with him and not dismiss his worries.

"I knew from the beginning that my second child was his opposite. My younger daughter is laid back and goes with the flow. She can handle a lot of things my son could not as an infant, such as missed or delayed naps, and she is more independent. I strive to follow peaceful and gentle parenting practices with both."

— Kate, 32, from Crown Point,
Indiana, parent of two children
(ages 3 years and 10 months)

Sensory threshold: In response to varied physical sensations, does your child react positively, negatively, or not at all? Some children are sensitive and easily overwhelmed by sensory input, such as noise, light, or textures, which makes crowded, noisy places difficult to navigate. Others will react in the opposite way and will seek out more stimulation on purpose.

Quality of mood: Does your child tend to be cheerful and upbeat or have a distrustful and serious demeanor? Your child's moods will of course vary from day to day, but in general, most children lean toward a more positive emotional state or a more negative one.

Human personalities are uniquely different, but all are beautiful and complementary. No matter where a child falls on the spectrum of each of these temperamental traits, she deserves to be understood and valued for who she is and who she is becoming. Certain situations will be easier for her to deal with, and some discipline strategies will work better for her than others. By understanding the way she approaches life's experiences, you will be able to empathize with her struggles, choose the most effective parenting techniques, and lovingly guide her toward adulthood.

Age-Appropriate Discipline

Your child's general temperament may stay fairly constant from infancy, but the natural course of human development is not a steady path. As your child grows older, his needs, interests, and behaviors will shift, sometimes dramatically, and therefore your discipline strategies must also cater to his present self, not to the child he was before.

Using the "distract and redirect" technique is often very effective and easy to implement for a 1-year-old, even if your child's temperament is fairly low in distractibility. However, a few years later, this same technique is not likely to go over well, as 4-year-olds have longer attention spans and a clearer understanding of how to follow rules. At age 3 and above, most children are able to make the connection between their actions and the natural consequences, but not before. Sparking the imagination is a technique that speaks especially to a 4-year-old's proclivity for pretend play, while a 1-year-old would just be confused.

In this book, you will find suggestions for techniques that generally work well for children at specific ages, given their current developmental capabilities.

Choose Your Approach

If I had to honestly describe my general approach to disciplining my own children, it would be fairly well encapsulated in these three words: patient, empathetic, and silly. As a highly emotional optimist, I often start the mornings with my young children by singing a familiar upbeat song, followed by raspberry-belly-induced giggling, and then a gentle reminder about the day's upcoming activities.

If one of my children begins to act out, I typically watch and wait first to see if my child will change his behavior on his own before I intervene, and I'm gifted at conveying my empathy. However, I do struggle with organization and routines. My spontaneous, impulsive personality can conflict with my children's need for structure. I may personally lean toward being a bit too messy and goofy, but

I strongly identify with other parents who use a gentle or positive approach to discipline.

Now it's your turn to craft your own approach to discipline. Your personality and outlook on life will greatly influence how you communicate with your child. Do you tend to be quieter or more boisterous? Do you enjoy flexibility or are you more rigid by nature? What is your tolerance for frustration? Do you typically see the glass as half-full or half-empty? Your child's temperament and age will also influence what disciplinary techniques are most effective. Finally, think about the long-term goals you consider most important to help your child learn right now. With these personal preferences in mind and the wide variety of techniques explained throughout this book, you will be on your way to creating a consistent philosophy of your own.

How to Use This Book

This book has been designed as a practical guide to understanding and managing your toddler's behavior. To help you navigate the transitions both into and out of toddlerhood, I have included information for a 4-year age span.

Each age-specific chapter of this book contains the following:

- An overview of your child's physical, cognitive, and social-emotional development
- Effective and age-appropriate discipline techniques
- Common behavioral issues with suggested strategies for overcoming them

Throughout the book, you will find sidebars and boxes with tips for navigating tricky situations, reminders of how to best communicate with your child, and advice from parents who have been in similar situations.

Keep in mind that child development is not a linear process. Your child may reach milestones sooner or later than another child who is the same age. The developmental notes are generalizations for each age group.

The suggested disciplinary techniques in this book do build upon one another from year to year. Each chapter's selections are particularly relevant for that age, but if you gradually learn how to use each year's tools, you will have a plentiful supply to pick and choose from throughout your child's toddlerhood. This flexibility will allow you to curate your own approach to discipline based on the needs of your child.

Specific behaviors also vary greatly depending on your child's temperament and other environmental factors. Some topics, such as sleep or tantrums, may appear in several chapters with age-specific advice. For example, tantrums may simply not be an issue for you until your child is past the age of 2, whereas another child may have severe tantrums as a 1-year-old and none by age 3. When a topic is not covered in one age group, it's perfectly fine to skip around either before or after your child's biological age to find strategies for specific behavioral issues.

In-Depth Look:
Be Your Own Sounding Board

Getting to the root of a challenging behavioral situation and deciding how to handle it requires objectivity—something of which all parents are in perpetual short supply! If you have a friend or willing partner to listen, that is a fantastic way to gain clarity. If not, you can be your own sounding board. Start by asking and answering these three big questions:

1. **Can I allow my child's current behavior to continue?**
    Only you can decide if the answer to this question is *yes* or *no*, but before you use any disciplinary technique, you need to know why you are choosing to allow the behavior or why you must stop it. There is so much to be said for letting things go unless you are fully ready and willing to follow through. Many of the challenging behaviors we see in our children have developmental reasons or are a sign of your child's temperament. If the activity in question is a reasonable one for the age of your child and isn't doing any real harm to anyone or anything, consider letting it go or changing the situation slightly so that you can allow it.

2. **Am I allowing for independence and providing security?** Many conflicts between adults and children occur because of the tension between the child's natural desire to acquire new skills, as modeled by the adults around him, and the desire for adult supervision and protection that will keep him safe as he explores. Effective parenting is never prescriptive. Like a scientist, before you come to a solution, you must observe, experiment, analyze, and then make changes if necessary.

3. **Am I focused on building a relationship based on trust and respect?** Take a close look at how you are responding to your child's behavior. Are you committed to nurturing a healthy relationship between the two of you? Disciplinary strategies that are belittling, threatening, manipulative, deceiving, coercive, or sarcastic may gain your child's obedience, but they will not gain your child's cooperation. Trust is earned, not demanded.

What you are aiming for is authentic, gentle loving guidance with clear limits. Answering these three questions will get you closer to that ideal.

CHAPTER TWO

1-Year-Olds

Your giggly, wobbly 1-year-old lives joyfully in the present moment. Easily distractible and driven by the need to hone gross motor skills, she may still seem more like a baby than a toddler especially in the beginning. However, about mid-year, new physical and cognitive abilities emerge, bringing with them different experiences and frustrations. Your primary job will be to keep her safe as she tests her newfound independence.

Development

Whether your child tends to be more boisterous or reticent, all 1-year-olds seek stimulation. They may make you laugh at their sheer unpredictability. This is the time when toddlers are caught throwing toys, dropping food on the floor, and playing with the trash can. As oddly unreasonable as your toddler's behavior may sometimes appear, the important thing to know is that it is always determined by her need for motor, sensory, language, and social-emotional development.

What's New?

From new words to first tantrums, this year is bound to be full of excitement and challenges. Your determined toddler will be growing rapidly and insisting on more freedom. If there is one overriding, defining characteristic of this age, it is the child's drive to accomplish gross motor skills.

With her first step, your child's entire view of the world changes. The ability to walk upright is a powerful and highly motivating accomplishment. Some children will already be walking by the beginning of this year, but if you still have a crawler, sit tight and have patience. It is not unheard of for a toddler to take until 18 months to begin walking as her primary mode of transportation. And once she masters this skill, she'll spend the next year refining it. Her next mission is to gain muscle strength as quickly as possible in order to learn to run, twist, catch, turn, and climb. This is also why 1-year-olds love lifting and lugging heavy objects, carrying them from one place to another. She is singularly focused on how good the movement feels.

The cognitive abilities of a 1-year-old are primarily impulsive and reactive. Her senses are highly attuned to her immediate surroundings, and as her prefrontal cortex is still largely undeveloped, she will not have access to foresight or logic. Curiosity is her greatest advantage when bumbling about, whether in her home or outdoors. She briefly explores every object she encounters with the hands and possibly the mouth, and then abandons it almost immediately for the next stimulating encounter. The ability to sustain focus on an activity for longer periods will emerge after she has a more thorough understanding of the world.

Throughout this year, she will be pointing at and gesturing toward all of the things that she finds fascinating, prompting you to name objects, give details, and explain what is happening. As you have these vocabulary-rich, primarily one-sided conversations, she will be listening much more than speaking. By 18 months, most toddlers can say at least 15 words. Regardless of how often your little one is talking this year, you will know that she is able to understand you by the way she engages with you, responding with excitement when you mention going somewhere she likes, such as Grandma's house, or bringing you items that you request. By the end of this year, most children can understand two-step commands such as "Go to your room and bring me your socks."

Without a doubt, the most empowering one-word phrase your child is likely to overuse this year, especially after the 18-month mark, has become a toddler cliché: it is, of course, the word *no*. Be assured that she's not trying to frustrate you—she is just showing off her new desire for independence. It's a milestone worth celebrating and a sign that she is ready to try some tasks on her own that you performed for her throughout babyhood.

Capabilities and Limitations

Understanding the general abilities and limitations of this age group will help you to remain patient when seeking to understand your child's behavior.

Lives in the here and now: Your toddler is acutely aware of the present moment, including all of the objects, people, and movement in his immediate vicinity. This innate mindfulness is a characteristic that many adults find admirable yet elusive, as thoughts of the future and regrets from the past interfere in the enjoyment of the here and now. What a gift it is for a young child to be able to focus so purely on the learning opportunities of the present moment! As parents, we can use this to our advantage as well. It is much easier to end a tantrum with a simple change of scene or the quick removal of an unsafe item. It is also a double-edged sword; there is no comfort in knowing that he can come back to the park and play tomorrow because to him, the concept of "tomorrow" does not exist yet.

Communicates nonverbally: Waving "bye-bye" is only one of the many gestures your 1-year-old is capable of. By now, she can communicate effectively through body language and facial expressions, even though she is not able to express herself very well through the spoken word. She is fairly adept at reading your moods as well, and then responding to or ignoring them as it suits her. Although she may understand how you feel about a certain situation, she does not have the reasoning skills to know why. For example, she knows that when she bites your arm you react with anger or sadness, but she is very confused as to why.

Understands simple, clear limits: When you say, "No," he definitely knows the meaning. It's just that the need to move and declare his independence is stronger than his need to please you. At this age, your toddler will continue to test boundaries until he finds a more satisfying outlet for his needs. It's best to make sure your firmest limits are used sparingly and to offer alternatives whenever possible.

Associates cause and effect: What happens when you go outside in the rain? Your skin gets wet and slippery and you can splash in puddles! These realizations will bring your toddler joy and help her learn to predict with greater accuracy what will happen the next time she repeats an action. While this is helpful, she still lacks the ability to transfer the knowledge and apply it consistently in a broader context. In other words, knowing that a puddle outside makes a big splash will not affect her decision to make a big splash in her own bathtub. She will be just as fascinated and will want to repeat every variation of an experience.

Insists upon independence: Your toddler has a new independent spirit and sense of self, and will take every opportunity to remind you that he now has opinions of his own. In fact, 1-year-olds are often contrarians for the sheer sake of being contrary! Knowing that independence is so important to him, you may be surprised when he exhibits the exact opposite: clinginess in new environments or separation anxiety when you're going away from him. At this age, your child may resist your limits strongly, but he still very much wants to be near you.

Communication

Some 1-year-olds are naturally more verbal than others, but even if you have a little chatterbox, true expressive verbal skills are far off in the future. Her *receptive* language skills, however, are fairly advanced. She can understand most simple directions and by now has acquired quite a large vocabulary. However, she will still be unable to tell you her thoughts and feelings, which can be very frustrating for her. She will have a clear idea of what she wants and is easily pacified if you show her that you understand. If you don't act quickly enough to meet her wants or needs, she is likely to fall back on the only thing that worked when she was a baby: crying.

Fortunately, the way you talk to her can have an enormously positive impact on your relationship. You will not be able to prevent all of her frustrations, but the number of tantrums can be significantly diminished, and life can be a whole lot more pleasant and joyful, when the two of you are on the same page.

When speaking to your young toddler, bend down to her level and look into her eyes. Stop all other body movements, unless you are specifically using sign language or other vocabulary-related gestures. This is an effective way to capture any child's attention; she is much more likely to hear and comprehend your words when she can see your lips moving and visually evaluate your facial expressions. Give your directions or information in short, simple phrases, and speak clearly and slowly. Sometimes even just saying a single word will help her focus on what you're asking her to do. Finally, make a good guess as to what she is feeling or wanting. By using these techniques, you are showing her respect. She is much more likely to respond positively if she knows that you are actively trying to help her.

Quick Tip: Avoid using baby talk when speaking to your child. The way he mispronounces words may be adorable, but his ears are listening for the correct pronunciation. Using real words and clearly spoken sentences conveys respect.

Age-Appropriate Discipline

Since the behavior of a 1-year-old is largely driven by physical and emotional needs, your job will be guiding your toddler toward developmentally appropriate activities while establishing and reinforcing clear limits. Children at this age should not be expected to comply just because you said so. Seek to understand your child's current capabilities and keep your expectations in check. Remember that all toddler behavior has an underlying purpose: to help the child grow into a more fully developed human being.

Create Child-Friendly Spaces

Be proactive and head off inappropriate behavior before it has a chance to happen by focusing on your child's surroundings. Start by evaluating the spaces your toddler spends the most time playing in. For many families, this could be a living room, dedicated playroom, bedroom, or even a kitchen. Look for any safety issues. Are there electrical outlets or blind cords that are easily exposed? Is the furniture, such as a shelf or heavy dresser, secured safely to the wall? Are there any choking hazards on the floor or breakable objects in an area where your child might climb and reach? Get down on all fours so that you are able to see what your child sees and eliminate any safety concerns.

Next, consider the overall feel of the space. Is it calm and peaceful, or loud and overstimulating? Is the TV often on in the background? Is there enough room to allow for gross motor movement? Does every toy have a clear place where it belongs? Reality check: Many parents find it difficult to organize toys, and this is because it is easy to acquire too many of them.

Finally, consider the accessibility of your child's toys and clothing. Is he able to reach what he needs himself without getting frustrated? While there is no reason to seek perfection, these environmental factors can affect your child's moods and activity levels. Even small tweaks to the play spaces can help ward off behavioral issues.

Quick Tip: Keep toy collections manageable by aiming for no more than 8 to 12 toys in a single play space. Try organizing them on a low shelf in baskets or bins rather than in a large toy chest.

Establish Consistent Routines

The ebb and flow of your daily activities can also affect your toddler's behavior and make certain transitions a lot easier. Start by imagining what the "perfect" day would look like for you and your toddler. What time would you ideally wake up? What would breakfast time feel like, and what happens next? Now, compare it with your current schedule. When you leave to go to work, do you have a good-bye routine that your toddler can anticipate? Do you sing a special lullaby just before bed?

When evaluating your current routine and comparing it with your ideal, consider whether your time frames are reasonable and if there are adequate transition cues for your toddler. Limit your child's choices and communicate with him so that he understands what is expected and what will happen next. For example, say, "When you are finished eating your snack, we will go outside to play."

Determine the Cause and Fulfill the Need

This year, you will be doing some detective work. The behavior of a 1-year-old can almost always be traced back to a physical or emotional need, but it may not be readily apparent. For example, a child who stumbles and falls down at the playground may cry because he has tripped and is hurt, or he may actually be showing signs that he is tired and is ready for a nap.

Common causes of emotional outbursts include physical discomfort—such as hunger, tiredness, being too hot or too cold, or overstimulation—and emotional discomfort—such as feeling insecure in a new environment or being uncomfortable with transitions. As you get to know your child's tolerance levels and personality, you will be able to pinpoint underlying issues with more accuracy. Sometimes giving your child a little snack or hug is all that is needed to set things right again.

Establish Boundaries

Learning how to respect oneself, others, and the environment begins as soon as a child realizes that she can affect the world around her. At age 1, your child is still innocently experimenting with cause and effect. She does not yet know that pulling the cat's tail or biting your arm causes pain. She does not understand that throwing a toy at a windowpane will cause it to shatter. She runs into the street because running feels good, as does exploring. It is up to you to determine what boundaries are most essential, and at this age, your child is not capable of understanding the complexity of polite social behavior. The limits you set for her must be simple, clear, and safety-focused.

Distract and Redirect

By now, your toddler fully understands the concept of object permanence: the knowledge that a hidden object is not truly gone, even when it is not in view. Even so, she will continue to enjoy peek-a-boo and hunting for her favorite toys throughout this entire year. She is highly distractible and has a short attention span when compared with older children. You can use this trait to your advantage when she is engaging in an unsafe or otherwise unacceptable behavior. When used properly, distraction and redirection is a respectful way of disciplining a young toddler.

In a calm and considerate tone of voice, briefly describe the problem with the current activity or behavior. Allow your child a moment or two so that you know she understands the limit you are placing on the previous activity. She may cry, push you away, ignore you, or throw a tantrum. Let her react to this news with her own emotions and accept her need to express her feelings, but try not to let too much time pass or overexplain your reasoning. Instead, immediately propose an alternative. The new activity may be a more acceptable form of the previous one or it may be entirely different. Toddlers this age often respond more to your actions and physical movements than your words, so don't be afraid to pick your child up and carry her into another room for a complete change of environment.

Here are just a few common behaviors for which the distraction and redirection technique could be useful.

Throwing a hard plastic toy: Because this behavior could hurt others or damage your home, it is not an acceptable way to practice throwing. You might tell your child, "This toy is not a good one for throwing. I'm going to put it back on the shelf now. Look what I found, though! Here is a soft ball that *is* good for throwing. Would you like to throw this?" Place the soft ball in your toddler's hands.

Digging in the trash can: Because it is unsanitary and potentially unsafe, you can't allow your toddler to continue. You might say, "The trash can is for garbage. Our hands stay out. I wonder what your hands might like to do instead. I have an idea. Maybe you would like to explore this basket of toys."

Crying for another cookie. No, she can't have as many cookies as she likes. Set that limit and suggest a different food or different activity. For example, you might say, "You already ate your cookie. I just saw a bird outside hopping around. Tweet, tweet! I love birds. Would you like to see the bird?"

Common Issues

Most everyone has a hiccup now and then—it's biologically normal. The issues you are facing with your 1-year-old's behavior are also biologically normal, and unlike the hiccups, there are lots of effective ways to handle them.

Tantrums

All humans have emotional outbursts. As we age, we can learn how to manage our frustrations, grief, or anger by channeling that negative energy into more productive outlets. But 1-year-olds do not have this ability yet. It is a life skill that comes from time, experience, and the gentle guidance of others.

In the context of this book, a "tantrum" is simply a big expression of big emotions. Your child trusts you enough to express his true feelings in front of you rather than keeping them bottled up inside. Your job is to help him learn better ways of managing his emotions. You can also use your compassion and gentle reassurance to connect with him emotionally, strengthening your relationship for the future. When you help your child make it through to the other side of a tantrum, you are giving him a gift for life.

What Causes Tantrums?

Babies are born with the instinct to cry in order to get their needs met. This is how they communicate to you that they are hungry, tired, wet, or in need of a cuddle. As your child passes from infancy into toddlerhood, she learns many other language and social-emotional skills to express her immediate needs and convey her moods, preferences, and desires.

However, when things don't go her way, she lacks the ability to effectively communicate what the problem is. Common tantrum triggers for this age include being hungry, not getting enough sleep or being ready for a nap, feeling overstimulated, craving more independence, experiencing a disruption in routine. Your 1-year-old has very little patience to wait for you to figure out the reason for her distress.

Her frustration may show itself in a burst of anxiety, sadness, or even anger. She might lie down on the floor, cry, kick, flail her arms, scream, or flop backward. When you have just watched your child playing happily moments ago, this sudden change can feel awkward or concerning. Know that this is normal 1-year-old behavior—she is not trying to manipulate you or test you. If you remain calm and patient, you can help her.

Prevent Tantrums from Starting

The good news: With some preparation, techniques that help you think on your toes, and a little bit of luck, it is possible to help your child avoid a tantrum. The preparation starts with your routines. Young children thrive on predictability and often are distressed by disruptions or the absence of objects in their usual place. By providing consistent routines and an organized environment at home, you are helping your child feel safe physically and emotionally.

The next step is to make a habit of regularly pausing to observe and evaluate your child's habits and emotional states. Is he getting enough sleep? Does he seem to get hungry at the playground after about an hour, or does he prefer to snack at home? What does he find most entertaining while waiting: verbal games, songs, toys, or books? Deterring a potential tantrum may be as simple as packing your diaper bag with a snack or toy or helping your child locate his shoes.

Most 1-year-old tantrums happen because your child lacks the communication skills to tell you what is wrong. If you can figure it out quickly and provide an immediate solution to fix the problem, this is the best form of tantrum prevention. In addition, if there is an unexpected event or you need to deviate from his usual routine, make sure to take the time to tell him what is going to happen. He will likely reward you with a calmer disposition.

Stop Tantrums

Let's face it: Because life is sometimes spontaneous and we must have reasonable boundaries, we can't always cater to our child's every need or desire. Children can get frustrated or upset even when we try our best to prevent it. If the tantrum is the result of a boundary you enforced, do not try to explain or reason with your 1-year-old. At this age, she is not capable of understanding logic, so this will only complicate things further. You might not be able to prevent your child's tantrums altogether, but by handling these emotional expressions with compassion and consistency, you can reduce their frequency and severity. What you need is a plan.

Find your calm. The first step in handling any behavioral issue is to keep your own emotions in check. Remember that you are the adult. If you are feeling angry or upset, pause for a moment to breathe deeply and get your own emotions under control. At this moment, your child is unable to manage her own feelings and you have all the power; before you can offer support and guidance, you need to be calm.

Empathize. Can you imagine how she is feeling right now? What is her body language communicating? Tell her in simple, clear-spoken words that you understand how she feels. If you can determine what it is she needs and you are able to supply it, the tantrum may end abruptly and with gratitude from your child. However, if she is in the middle of an outburst, she might not be able to hear you.

Comfort and reassure. Many 1-year-olds will calm down with physical reassurance. Try putting her in your lap to cuddle, gently rubbing her back, or offering a hug. Breastfeeding toddlers may find nursing a natural technique for self-soothing. Singing a lullaby or murmuring reassuring phrases like "I love you so much" can also work wonders. However, some children prefer not to be touched during an outburst. Try not to take offense if your child rebuffs your efforts, but don't walk away. Stay close by.

Wait. Have patience and allow her the time she needs to release these big emotions. If you are in public and you need to carry your child to a more private space to ride the tantrum out, go ahead and do it, but it is important not to rush this part of the process. Trust that this wave of emotion will rise up and fall back down naturally.

Use Your Words: Everyone needs to feel understood. When empathizing with your child during a tantrum, try this simple phrase to get the message across. "You are feeling [state the emotion] because [state the cause]." For example, "You are feeling angry because you really wanted to play with that lamp."

Recover from a Tantrum

When the big emotions subside, it's time to reconnect and move on. How you choose to recover will depend on your location, the time of day, and your child's personality. After a short-lived tantrum, you may have good results with the "distract and redirect" technique. If the tantrum occurred in a grocery store, for example, the natural next step may be to continue shopping. If you are at home indoors, you can go outside for a change of scenery.

However, your child might not be ready to move on yet. Making it through a long and difficult tantrum can be exhausting. A slower transition back to normalcy will allow both of you to process what happened and regain emotional balance. He might want to sit in your lap and cuddle while you hum a tune, read a story, or fiddle with a toy. This special bonding moment after a tantrum can be an opportunity for honesty and affection. Reaffirm how much you love him, recount the lessons learned, and even apologize if you feel it's necessary. And when you feel the moment is right, make a suggestion for moving on with the day.

Remember that taking the extra time to fully heal any emotional wounds and focus on a loving connection will pave the way for shorter, less time-consuming tantrums in the future.

Sleeping

Everyone's mood is improved when they feel well-rested, but getting a good night's sleep can sometimes be difficult for both parents and their toddlers. On average, 1-year-olds need about 13 to 14 hours of total sleep, including daytime naps and nighttime rest. Unfortunately, there are many factors that can interfere with your child's sleep that are beyond your control, including growth spurts, illnesses, disruptions in routines, and developmental phases.

Fortunately, it is possible to anticipate the rough patches and address underlying issues. Since many behavioral challenges occur because of inadequate amounts of sleep, establishing healthy sleep habits should be a high priority for all families with young children.

Why Sleep Is Important

If you go to a playground and wait long enough, you are likely to see a fussy toddler and a parent sighing heavily, mumbling apologetically about how "it must be nap time" or "last night was a rough one." Parents can often observe the connection between sleep and behavior in their children. Children who do not get adequate sleep may show irritability, physical aggression, and—although it may seem a contradiction—hyperactivity. If the sleep deprivation is severe, it can have long-term effects on a child's ability to concentrate, disrupting his natural growth and development. A happy, well-rested child will have more energy and motivation to practice new skills than a sleepy, cranky one.

Tantrums are a normal part of toddlerhood, but if your child seems grouchier or more hyper than usual, overtiredness could be the cause. The solution? Assess whether his needs are being met in the sleep department and, if necessary, make a change in his routine.

Bedtime Struggles

Have you ever been to a fun party and left earlier than the other guests? Even though you know you need to get to work early the next morning, you may regret having left the fun behind. You also might be hyped up for a while, unable to sleep. A version of this happens to toddlers, too. If your child begins running wildly, babbling animatedly, or even crying loudly just as she should be settling down for sleep, she may be experiencing the Fear of Missing Out.

The moment your child discovers her new independent spirit, she may decide it is worth fighting for. As the responsible adult, you are in control of nearly every aspect of her life, and have been since she was born—from what food is served to the objects she is or is not allowed to play with. Actual bodily functions, such as sleeping, eating, and toileting, are things she can exert her control over, so bedtime struggles are common for toddlers. While you can't make her go to sleep, you can create a soothing sleeping space and a consistent routine that is more satisfying than the urge to defy you.

Pay careful attention to your bedtime routine. Don't miss that sleepy window! Involve her in a wind-down routine well in advance of her real nap or bedtime to avoid overtired hyper behavior. Allow her to make choices and exert her desire for independence along the way. For example, let her try brushing her own hair and teeth before you assist. Let her pick out the story for you to read. Feel free to experiment with a variety of routines, but after you pick one, stay extremely consistent. Breastfeeding parents may choose to nurse their toddlers to sleep, and this is a perfectly fine part of a sleep routine as long as it is consistently offered. Any deviation from the norm will invite a struggle, so be clear on your routine. Finally, make sure that her sleeping area is darkened and relatively unstimulating.

Night waking is also a common issue at this age. Just as when she was a baby, your toddler may wake up at night because she is hungry, wet, or needs help settling back down to sleep. It may be difficult for an exhausted parent to hear, but "sleeping through the night" does not mean that your child will go to bed and sleep straight through until the morning. She will be entering and exiting sleep in biologically predetermined sleep cycles, and at the end of each one is a natural and normal brief period of wakefulness. It is at this point that she might cry out in the middle of the night. If she is not really and truly awake, but instead is briefly exiting one of these sleep cycles, she might go right back to sleep. Comfort objects, such as a special blanket or small plush toy, may be helpful for this purpose. However, if she is truly awake and cries for you, go attend to her.

Keep the room dark and rub her back, nurse, rock, or do whatever feels natural to you to offer comfort. You can also set some boundaries, however: If your child is waking up often to feed and you are ready to curb this habit, you might consider nursing or feeding her just before bed and telling her that she may nurse or eat food again in the morning. This can be a difficult part of parenting, but your compassionate and consistent approach to bedtimes and night waking will help your child learn that she is safe and secure at night.

Sleeping Alone

If you love sleeping in the same bed with your 1-year-old and everyone is feeling well-rested, there's no need to change your current routine. Not everyone feels this way, though, and if you are ready to transition your child from your bed to his own, there are a few steps you can take to make it happen with minimal distress.

Pick the bed. You may prefer using a crib, especially if your little one is closer to 12 months, or you may put a mattress directly on the floor or use a low toddler bed with side rails properly installed. Most children make the transition to a "big kid" bed sometime between 18 months and 3 years.

Do a safety check. Since 1-year-olds are explorers, even at night, you will need to make sure that the room and all other accessible areas are prepared with safety in mind. Secure all furniture to the wall and consider installing a baby gate to prevent your child from exploring unsafe areas at night.

Decide on an approach. Think about how you will make this transition. Will you go cold turkey? Will you do a gradual shift? You could temporarily put his small bed next to yours or lie next to him in his own bed for a few weeks. Consider the potential use of comforting objects or a blanket to cuddle. Some families prepare the sleeping room with a few toys so that the child can play for a little bit during a pre-sleep wind-down time.

Be compassionate. Remember that establishing a new routine can be stressful for a young child. It may take a couple of months for this transition to be completed, and there may be a little bit of crying as your child expresses his discomfort. Your child will eventually learn how to go to sleep independently.

Stay the course. Be sympathetic and attentive, but don't give in now and then just because it's tough. Inconsistency will make the process longer and more traumatic for everyone.

Eating

In the span of one year, your baby tripled her birth weight, and she had to eat every few hours to get enough calories to accomplish this physical growth. Toddlers grow much more slowly, and they do not need to eat as frequently or as much as they used to. In addition, the child herself controls whether she eats at all—and she knows it! She will experiment with independence by choosing how much to eat and what foods she finds palatable to swallow. It's easy for parents and toddlers to allow mealtime to become a point of contention. Providing some freedom within limits will eliminate the food battles.

Helping a Picky Eater

Using threats, wheedling, negotiating, or bribing children to eat has the exact opposite effect. When children feel cornered or coerced, they will be even *less* compliant. If you have a picky eater, it is important that you have realistic expectations and take a more relaxed approach. Try these strategies to eliminate any mealtime conflict.

Encourage Independence: Allow your toddler to help with the food preparation. Even young toddlers will benefit from shared sensory experiences while you cook. She will not have the skills to chop, but she can transfer items from one bowl to another with her hands. Help her drop a few coarsely chopped veggies into the bowl or mash her little fingers into the kneaded dough. Your older toddler will be ready for more advanced skills. A small jam-spreading knife without a sharp edge is perfect for slicing soft foods like bananas or cooked sweet potatoes. When possible, let her serve herself a portion of food onto her own plate. Make sure she can access everything she needs for a meal, including her plate, bowl, cup, and utensils. Give your child a small pitcher to pour her own water to drink. Show her where to put her empty plate when she is finished and how to clean up any spills. By giving her direct opportunities to assert her independence throughout mealtime, she may feel less of a need to engage in a battle over the food itself.

Offer a variety: Rather than catering to your child's specific food preferences, make sure that the food you serve represents a wide variety of healthy choices. Many children will eat more when given small amounts of many different foods on a plate rather than only one single food choice. When your toddler consistently rejects a certain food, do not stop offering it. Continue to make it available, but don't pressure her in any way to eat it. Sometimes children need to see and taste a food many times before they decide it is something they enjoy.

Model healthy eating behavior: When you share mealtimes, you can model the behavior you'd like to see from your child. Make time to sit down and allow your child to watch as you serve yourself food and drink. Make an obvious show of polite manners such as having conversation and using a napkin or wiping up spills as you eat. Talk about your food choices and why you enjoy them. Describe the textures and flavors with enthusiasm. When you are finished, you might even sometimes intentionally leave a bit of food on your plate, mentioning that you are full and will save the rest of the food for later—this will show that that food ingestion should be determined by hunger and not by what has been served.

Staying Healthy

Just because your child is picky about a certain food or preparation today does not mean that he will feel the same way tomorrow. Validate for him that everyone has likes and dislikes, and that he is in charge of what foods he eats today. Use positive language and make sure you are authentically encouraging his new decision-making skills, not trying to manipulate him into eating something specific.

If your child is refusing to eat vegetables, there is no need to sneak them into food. If your child discovers that you are doing this behind his back, he may stop trusting the foods you offer him altogether. However, there are many ways you can cook with healthier foods, such as adding spinach to a smoothie or incorporating extra vegetables into a family favorite recipe. Instead of sneaking, involve your child in the integration and preparation of these healthy foods.

As part of your family's healthy food plan, it is important to limit or eliminate foods that are low in nutritional value, such as juice, candy, or other "junk" foods. Decide ahead of time when and how many sweets are reasonable. Never use them as rewards for good behavior. Instead, treat them like any other food option, except that this type of food is limited in supply.

By making whole, unprocessed foods the mainstay of your child's diet and taking the external pressures off of eating in general, you will set the stage for a healthy relationship to food for life.

Quick Tip: You'll find that 1-year-olds love to explore cause and effect and often make a mess while eating, including dropping or slinging food. Limiting the amount of food on your child's plate at one time will naturally make this less of a problem. This behavior also may be an indication that she is finished eating and is ready for playtime instead. When this happens, ask if she is finished eating and then quickly move on to the next activity. Distraction and redirection work well here—you can give her more appropriate objects with which to practice dropping and throwing skills away from the eating area.

Physical Aggression

Even if you have only ever modeled kind and gentle interactions, your child may go through periods of physical aggression that you will need to address. Someday, she will be able to use her words and understand the nuances of appropriate social engagement, but right now her verbal communication skills are severely limited. It may help to remember that at this age, your child is still *innocent*, no matter what her behavior is showing you.

Why Toddlers Hurt Others

It is in fact your child's job to test boundaries, explore sensations, and try to get your attention in ways that adults often perceive as negative or bad behavior. This includes using her body in forceful ways. A 1-year-old is not capable of purposefully trying to hurt you or anyone else. If she is hurting others, whether it's yanking your pet's tail, swatting at your face, pushing another child, or biting your arm, there is a reason for her actions.

Addressing this need is part of the solution. Is she biting because her gums hurt from teething? Could she possibly be hungry? If so, you can solve those problems right now by providing a snack or other object that is safe to chew on. If the bite is a result of her frustration, the solution is a little more nuanced. It will require your full attention and communication skills. Remember to always lean down low, look into your child's eyes, and speak without judgment.

Stop the Hurting

When your child is engaging in hurtful behavior, your first job is to not overreact. By showing your fear, frustration, or anger, you are sending your child a message that invites a battle. If you are feeling upset, take a deep breath and steel your expression. Your face needs to look calm and concerned. Your voice needs to convey confidence and authority.

Next, intervene and put a stop to the aggressive behavior. Since 1-year-olds often do not follow verbal directions, you will need to use your own body. Sometimes this will be easy to do. For example, if your child is pulling your pet's tail, you might put your own body between your child and your pet. You can say, "That hurts Kitty," and redirect by modeling how to use a gentle petting motion instead. Gentle redirection should be your go-to response, since it often works very well with this age group, and with this technique you could easily end up with a beaming child proudly patting the cat gently.

Continues on page 44

In-Depth Look: Addressing Underlying Causes

Even if you keep calm and respectfully intervene every time, a behavior may continue to happen until the underlying cause is resolved. You may need to steadily keep intervening over and over, because at this age once often isn't enough to change a child's behavior. Look at all the possible reasons for the action and be proactive in redirecting your child to more acceptable behaviors. We'll use the tail-pulling incident described on the previous page as an example, but this approach also applies to biting, pinching, hitting, kicking, scratching, or any other physically aggressive behavior.

Cause and effect: The last time she pulled Kitty's tail, there was an interesting effect and it was exciting: Kitty meowed. As a result, your little one learned that she could have a direct effect on the world around her. Look for other ways for her to explore this. For example, does Kitty meow when being fed or purr when petted? Draw her attention to these actions and reactions instead.

It feels good: The softness of Kitty's tail is enticing. Perhaps you can put Kitty in your lap and show her how to pet an animal gently so that she has a positive sensory experience. Also, make sure that your child has something appropriate to pull, such as a pull-toy.

Frustration: Kitty keeps frantically running away from her, and she can't understand why! Unable to communicate this frustration verbally, she tries to assert dominance over her pet. Show her that you understand by vocalizing this feeling for her. "Kitty is running away from you. That is making you feel sad."

Attention: Despite her attempts to get her pet to play with her, Kitty is choosing to ignore the situation by refusing eye contact and flicking his tail in annoyance. Surely pulling the tail will get Kitty to look at her. Stand up for your pet's right to not be a child's toy. Give her some information: "Kitty does not want to play. He wants to be alone. But I want to play peek-a-boo! Will you find me?"

Continued from page 41

However, 1-year-olds can be persistent. If your child ignores your redirection and requires a firmer intervention, continue to block your child's physical actions by saying firmly, "I will not let you hurt Kitty," or "Kitty doesn't like that." You can then remove your pet from your child's area, or you can remove your child from your pet's area. If you remove your child, you will need to go with her. Either solution will make your point. You also need to realize that enforcing this limit may frustrate your child, and you may be headed into tantrum territory (see page 27 for how to handle a tantrum). Either way, it is up to you to prevent your child from physically harming others.

Non-Compliance

You say, "Come over here," and your child runs away as fast and far as his little wobbly legs will take him. You say, "Eat your broccoli," and he looks right at you with a grin while dropping the food onto the floor. Any potential efforts to control him are easily rebuffed with cries of "No!" or "Go away!" He might even resist you with quite a bit of muscle strength, throwing his head or whole body backward at unexpected times. Screeching is also not uncommon!

It is this behavior that causes many parents to insist that they have a child who is especially "strong willed." Facing opposition from your child can be an unsettling and humbling experience. Is letting your child do things "his way" a sign of *bad parenting*? Is it time to lay down the law and insist on obedience? Actually, non-compliance is a good sign that your child is experimenting with self-determination, his new ability to make choices and insist on a more independent way of life.

Keeping Your Toddler Safe

A good rule of thumb is to say *yes* to your toddler as often as possible and reserve your *no* for the times when you really do need to demand his compliance for his own safety or the safety of others. Very often, 1-year-olds can be dangerously impulsive. Since their brains lack maturation in the prefrontal cortex, they are unable to understand logic or reasoning like an adult. Setting limits on unsafe behavior, however, is your responsibility as the supervising adult.

It is a great help to address potential problem areas before they even happen. Make a plan for how you will handle certain situations and be consistent with your routine. For example, before crossing a busy street, you might say to your child, "It is my job to keep you safe. You will either hold my hand or ride in the stroller while we cross the street." After crossing, empathize with your child and thank him for complying. Other common safety issues for 1-year-olds include escaping from the house, getting buckled into a car seat, and grabbing sharp or dangerous objects such as knives or electrical cords. Do what you can to prepare child-friendly spaces (see page 23) and then insist on absolute compliance for these really important safety issues.

Gaining Cooperation

For all other non–safety-related issues, you may be able to give your child a bit of leeway so she can embrace her independence. By focusing on the word *yes,* you are essentially telling your child that you respect her need to do things her way and you value her feelings and opinions. Here are a few common situations in which 1-year-olds are often uncooperative and some possible solutions that celebrate the ability to make choices for oneself.

Diaper changes: For quick changes, try changing her diaper while she's standing up rather than lying down. She may feel empowered by the new, confident position. Involve her in the process as much as possible. She may be happier to be changed if she is the one to pick out a diaper and help put it on. Distracting her with a silly song or a special "diaper change only" toy can also be helpful.

Getting dressed: Try picking out her clothes the day before and putting them in a special basket so that she knows exactly where to find them instead of rummaging in the closet or drawer every day. Make a game out of it by asking her to bring you each item from the basket one by one. Alternatively, allow extra time for her to try putting on her clothes herself.

Cleanliness: It can be difficult to get your child's cooperation while cleaning up. Again, try to encourage independence. Show your child her food-covered face in the mirror and give her a washcloth to wipe it herself. Model washing your hands after playing outside. Offer items for self-care, like a toothbrush (keep the toothpaste away for now), hairbrush, washcloth, or an unbreakable mirror.

Use Your Words: Note that while encouraging independence is the best way to gain cooperation, sometimes the hair *must* be washed or the nose wiped. As the adult, you always reserve the right to make the final call. Say calmly and emphatically, "I am going to help you now. I know that you don't like it, but it needs to happen. I will be fast, and then it will be done." Stay true to your words!

Toileting

Let's lay it right out: There is no perfect time to help your child learn to use the toilet. The age when parents transition their children out of diapers depends largely on cultural expectations. In some families, babies are diaper-free right from birth and the toileting process is a continuation of how they have been communicating with their children all along. I am not going to address this method in this chapter. Instead, we are focusing on how you can cultivate a healthy awareness of the toileting process.

Developing Awareness

Your child has already begun the toileting process this year, whether you have formally acknowledged it or not. Every time you change his diaper, he becomes aware of the association between his body functions and the result: a wet or poopy diaper. This is a feeling that is as comforting to him as any other routine you established when he was a baby. Learning to use the toilet with confidence starts with both your readiness and his as you help him learn a new habit.

As soon as your child begins walking, you can start helping him become more aware of his body. While some adults find the topic of poop uncomfortable, your child does not. He approaches this subject in just the same way as he learns about the world around him. This is the time to tell him the real names of all of his body parts and encourage his independence in the diaper-changing process (see page 46). He may want to be with you while you are using the toilet yourself, and while you may find the lack of alone time frustrating, this type of modeling is healthy for your child. If he expresses interest, it's also fine to give him a little potty of his own to sit on for fun and role-play, just as he might engage in pretend play with other household objects.

Speaking of play, during this same period, you may find your toddler playing in the bathroom by pulling the toilet paper, climbing in the sink, or dropping items in the toilet. This bit of mischief-making is common. Since you want your child to have positive feelings in this area of your home, try not to make a big deal out of it. Redirect toward more appropriate playful activities, such as dragging a pull-toy or dropping a soft toy into a bucket.

Ready or Not?

If your child is younger than 18 months, you may have some early success (and possibly subsequent regression), but most parents find that young toddlers lack the communication skills to tell you when they need to pee or poop. They also lack the physical skills to get to the toilet in time with clothes off or pulled down, which can be an obstacle.

All children develop at different rates, so of course no one can tell when you and your child will be ready. Most children have the awareness, interest, language skills, and physical capabilities to be successful somewhere between 2 and 3 years old, with some falling a little before or after that range. If you feel your child might be ready, feel free to read more about this topic in chapter 3, where you will find how-to details and tips for ensuring success (see page 74).

Parent to Parent:
When It Doesn't Work the First Time

"Of course, his awareness started much earlier with the opportunities we gave him to participate in his own care and his exploration of the bathroom, but we started the 'official' toileting process when he was 16 months old with lots of patience and modeling. The problem was that he just wasn't ready. After two days in without a single 'catch' on the toilet, we stopped and went back to cloth diapers.

"Several months later, I sensed a new level of general awareness in him. Thinking he might be ready, we tried a second time. We ditched diapers and went naked bottom for a few days, then commando. Amazingly enough, he learned to use the toilet consistently within a couple of weeks. He quite literally trained himself.

"We didn't need any bribes or punishments—he was just ready, and it was a breeze. I know that, had we pushed for it earlier, the whole process would have taken much longer and had more bumps along the way."

— Amy, 30, from Wichita,
Kansas, parent of two children
(ages 5 and 3 years)

CHAPTER THREE

2-Year-Olds

L ife with your 2 year old may feel like an emotional roller-
coaster ride: joyful and agreeable one minute and angry and
defiant the next. His temperament will play a large part in whether
these ups and downs are mild and easily dealt with or utterly
exhausting. Your ability to identify developmental characteristics
and then wait patiently and compassionately for them to pass will
also make an enormous difference.

Development

You'll find that 2-year-olds can be very intense. The urge to engage
in physical activity is still just as compelling as ever, but by now,
your child is stronger and her movements are more refined. She
wanders over to investigate interesting items with more intention,
trying to figure out the relevance and usefulness of the object.

Body parts and body functions are especially fascinating,
leading to a more conscious effort on her part to transition from
diaper to toilet. She is still impulsive and possessive, and even when

she knows where you have set the boundaries on her behavior, she may defy you in order to satisfy her curiosity. At other times, she seems to crave your affection and returns it with beatific smiles in lingering moments of tenderness, perhaps even petting your arm or leg before melting into your lap.

What's New?

Parents often describe the rambunctious energy of a 2-year-old as similar to having a "little tornado" in the house. It's often easiest to captivate your toddler's attention through big movements, like jumping, running, and climbing. These are skills he worked hard to master over the last year, and this year his body still needs to repeat them daily. By now, he can kick and throw a ball, stand on tiptoe, and walk up and down the stairs if he holds onto a handrail.

His fine motor skills are a bit slower to develop, but most 2-year-olds are able to do more than scribble on a piece of paper. Straight lines and circles emerge in his artwork. Puzzles and open-ended toys that can be stacked, transferred, twisted, sorted, and counted may hold great appeal. Sensory experiences continue to entice and entertain.

Depending on his personality, communicating with others might be a bit easier than it was last year. Most 2-year-olds speak in short two- to four-word phrases or sentences. When in a calm and agreeable mood, your child may be able to communicate what he needs. However, if he is experiencing frustration, this ability may disappear in the heat of the moment.

Socially, 2-year-olds are self-absorbed, tending to engage more in parallel (side-by-side) play than cooperative play. Expecting them to altruistically share toys and take turns is unrealistic at this stage of development. Your child will need your help in protecting his right to possess a toy while he is playing with it, and in following through when it is someone else's turn to play with it and he is upset.

Quick Tip: Young children often have occasional aversions to or extra interest in sensory experiences. The best way to handle this is to respect your child's preferences and be patient. Forcing tho iscuo may cause more frustration for everyone. If, however, you suspect your child's sensory intensity or social communication skills are outside of the normal range, talk to his doctor. There are a groat number of sensory-stimulating or desensitizing activities that you can do regularly together to help decrease his frustrations.

Capabilities and Limitations

Demonstrates assertiveness: Your 2-year-old is much more capable of taking care of her own needs now, and she knows it. She won't hesitate to try the things she sees you doing without asking you for help; if you tell her "No" often, she will perceive you as a barrier and will intentionally defy your rules. A small percentage of children this age even sneak behind your back and tell a lie or two (see page 134 for how to handle lies). To avoid excessive mischief-making in your cabinets or closets, keep her supplies down low where she can reach them and ask for her involvement in your daily routines.

Understands personal possessions: At this age, she is motivated primarily by her own desires, and she begins to understand that certain items, such as toys or pieces of food, can belong to her alone. When she yells, "Mine!" it is a good sign that this concept is sinking in. While it may cause aggressive behavior in social situations (such as when she's unwilling to share a toy), she will soon understand that if one can possess an item, it can also be freely given to another out of love or compassion. Allow her the opportunity to revel in these wonderfully fierce emotions, and be her guide by playfully practicing turn-taking.

Plays make-believe: You may hear her talking to herself as she engages in pretend play, emulating the tasks she sees you doing in your daily life, such as cooking, working with tools, or shopping. However, she is developmentally unable to distinguish fantasy from reality, which means that cartoon characters, mythological creatures, monsters, Santa Claus, and anthropomorphic animals in stories all feel equally real (and possibly frightening) to her. Keep her grounded in reality by reassuring her about what's real and what's pretend. When she asks, always tell her a simple version of the truth.

Seeks sensory experiences: Most 2-year-olds enjoy quite a bit of messy play. Your child may be drawn to playing with water, mud, playdough, paint, and any other sticky, squishy stuff she can get her hands on. She may also have clear and emphatic preferences about which textures she likes or dislikes, including food and clothing. Her attention span for these activities is short, so don't expect sustained concentration. Instead, have lots of opportunities for her to stimulate her senses that involve minimal and easy cleanup. If you find her in your kitchen covered in flour or syrup, you'll know that she has an unfulfilled need for this kind of messy play.

Communication

For now, you are in charge of clarifying expectations and empathizing with your child's emotions. He is incapable of seeing the world from your perspective. All behavioral issues will be resolved much more quickly and effectively if you first accept that your child will occasionally be disrespectful, ill-tempered, and possibly physically aggressive. Put your own ego aside, and then spend some time learning to speak in a way your toddler can understand.

First, assess your child's emotional state. Is he expressing joy? Sadness? Anger? Surprise? Frustration? Look at all of his facial and body cues, from bared teeth to hunched shoulders. Now, get down low and give him your full attention. Make your own body a mirror of his as you verbalize what you see. "You are crying. Your hands are in fists."

Then, make a guess as to how your child is feeling and why. When you speak, keep the volume low, but make the tone of your voice match the emotion. "You feel mad! You wanted to go outside. You are angry because I wouldn't let you play in the rain." This unique manner of speaking may feel odd at first, but with practice, it will become second nature. Often, after feeling completely understood, toddlers will calm down on their own and be receptive to your suggested solutions or redirection.

Age-Appropriate Discipline

It isn't easy to be a 2-year-old, compelled to touch, taste, and possess nearly everything in the environment, even when it isn't safe, respectful, or healthy to do so. Her impulsive nature also makes delayed gratification very difficult. Fortunately, as the adult, you can give her appropriate outlets while keeping her safe from danger. Your child needs you to empathize with her current moods, give her clear boundaries, model appropriate behaviors, and intervene in ways that foster her developing independence rather than preventing it.

Say "Yes"

How often do you restrict your child's activities or behaviors because they are unreasonable, irritating, or disruptive? If you're not sure, get a piece of paper and make a checkmark every time your response is "No." If the checkmarks seem excessive by the end of the day, you may want to evaluate how you can say "Yes" instead.

Many times, you may be able to provide a positive alternative by creating a new opportunity for action or redirecting to a different activity altogether. For example, if your child grabs a fragile object and bangs it on the floor, instead of saying, "No," affirm your child's need for exercising the arm muscles, saying, "Banging is fun. Yes, you may bang. Let's find something that isn't breakable." By saying "Yes" as often as possible, even to the things that are mildly irritating, our children will learn to trust that we are looking out for their best interests when we do set those limits.

Offer Limited Choices

Letting your child choose between two acceptable options can be an effective discipline technique. When you give him simple choices, such as whether to wear the red shirt or the blue shirt, you are empowering him to make decisions for himself. Asking for someone's opinion is considerate and respectful. Just don't be surprised when he practices his decision-making skills by choosing his favorite, only to quickly reject it in favor of the other option.

However, having too much freedom will have the opposite effect, causing your child to feel stressed and insecure. If he is given an entire closet full of shirts to choose from, he may well toss them all out and play in them, unable to cognitively handle all of the complicated choices.

As much as he needs to have some say in his life, he also needs you to show that you are ultimately in control. This helps him to feel safe and protected as he explores decision-making and problem-solving. Do him a favor and pare down his options in advance.

Be Consistent and Follow Through

Because she is learning social boundaries, it is your child's job to push to see if you will change your mind. She's not trying to manipulate you. She's really just trying to figure it all out. Therefore, it is your job to make sure that when you establish a routine, you stick to it as much as possible. If she asks, and the answer is "No," there should be no waffling, whining, or conceding. She needs you to mean what you say and follow through with calm consistency.

Since no family will have the exact same routine or expectations for what is allowable, you will need to first decide what your limits are and also how you will enforce them. For example, if your general rule during mealtime is that food stays on the table, you will need to supervise your child closely during this time. If your child tries to take the food elsewhere, it is your job to always respectfully intervene. You might respond with a simple choice by asking, "Do you want to eat some more or are you ready to wash your hands? When you stand up, that tells me you are finished. I will help you go wash your hands." After your child makes the choice, you need to make sure you are not being pulled back into a game or battle of wills. Affirm that the choice has been made, acknowledge feelings, and stay true to your word.

Be Playful and Physical

Certainly there will be times when you need to have your serious "I mean business" face on when setting a limit, but remember that the more you bring joy into your parenting strategies, the more positive behaviors you will see. Toddlers need to feel your love and devotion through playful movement and physical affection.

There are so many fun ways to encourage compliance. When offering your child a piece of broccoli, why not sing a silly song about healthy vegetables? During a transition period where you need to get her peacefully from the playground to the car, why not play airplane one day and "fly" there instead of walking? Is your little monkey jumping on the bed? Put a cushion or two on the floor and jump with her while chanting the rhyme. Facing a teeth-brushing battle? Perhaps she'd be happy to play along if you're brushing her "alligator teeth." When all else fails, sometimes a romping chase around the house is just exactly the energetic emotional release that she needs. Give in to the temptation and embrace your silly side— even if just for a minute or two.

Remove Your Child from the Situation

Toddlers may not be able to stop themselves from repeating an inappropriate behavior, even when redirected. Dangerous or hurtful behavior must be stopped immediately and prevented from happening again. The best thing to do when you are in this situation may be to physically remove either the object from your child's view or your child from the situation entirely. Do not spend any extra time giving choices, wheedling, or bargaining. Since a 2-year-old often will not willingly walk out of a tense situation, you will need to pick him up and carry him. This technique is especially useful if you are in a public area, such as a grocery store, and your child is on the verge of a tantrum. Instead of handling the issue in front of an audience, you both might feel more comfortable addressing your emotions in a neutral zone, away from the place of conflict.

You can also use this technique on yourself. If you are feeling angry or out of control, and your child is already in a safe space under the supervision of another adult, you may find that removing yourself from the situation is helpful.

Note that removal should never be used to isolate or punish a child for misbehavior. What you are doing here is *taking a break* together so that you can resolve the problem and emotionally reconnect. Instead of giving your child a "time-out," which breeds resentful feelings and is rather meaningless to him, you are creating a safe place to work through the issue. If your child has a tantrum after removal, he may be confused afterward about what happened. Make sure to acknowledge his feelings and express your love for him. When you are both calm and ready, you can go back and try again or you might suggest a different activity altogether.

Common Issues

Some days may be terrible, but they don't all have to be! Here are some tips for taming those 2-year-old tantrums and handling the messy spills, among other common issues, you might be facing this year.

Tantrums

Last year, your child spent much of her time strengthening her muscles through physical activity. She is much stronger now, and if she has tantrums when she is overly tired, frustrated, or hungry, they may be longer and more difficult to stop once they start. A 2-year-old can scream louder, kick harder, and cry longer.

That said, a tantrum doesn't have to be a big deal when you know how to weather the storm. The basic strategies for handling tantrums will remain the same as last year (see page 27), but this year, it will be especially important for you to model appropriate methods for handling your own frustration and to choose the right time during a tantrum to problem-solve.

Be a Good Role Model

It's not just children who have tantrums—even adults have bad days. It's a normal part of human life to get grouchy and lose your temper occasionally. It's also not unheard of for an adult to yell, stomp around, cry, or lie down in exasperation. Your 2-year-old is not able to understand why he gets upset or the best way to handle it, but he is watching and learning from you. When you lose your cool by yelling or acting physically aggressive toward yourself or others in front of your child, you are sending him a direct message: When you get upset, you can demonstrate your feelings through out-of-control, aggressive behavior.

The next time you feel frustration bubbling up in the presence of your child, try talking out loud about your feelings and actions as you help yourself calm down in a positive manner. This is not always possible, of course, but if you make a habit of it, you will be resetting your own automatic responses to intense feelings. For example, if you suddenly realize that you are missing a major ingredient in the middle of cooking dinner, you might say, "I'm feeling very upset right now because I don't have one of the ingredients for this recipe. I'm angry that I forgot to buy it when I was at the store last week. I need to take a break and calm down first before I decide what to do. I am going to take some deep breaths and sit here on the couch for a minute." While 2-year-olds are characteristically self-absorbed, they may show concern and offer a hug. In this situation, you are sending another direct message: When you get upset, you can calm yourself down and accept help from others.

When you sense that your child is bordering on frustration, try using the same positive calm-down language you use in your modeling. For example, if your child is getting exceptionally frustrated with a puzzle, you might say, "You are twisting the puzzle piece, but it is not going into the right slot. You are frowning and shaking your head." After describing the situation, you might suggest that he put the puzzle away for now and take a break. Remind him of the day when you were frustrated and he offered you a hug. Ask him if a hug might make him feel better. With your modeling and reminders, he will learn that there are better ways to express frustration than to have a tantrum.

Taming Tantrums

A child who is screaming, physically lashing out, or crying is suffering. While always empathizing with her, you will also need to work to help her shorten the duration of her outbursts. Once a tantrum has started, it typically progresses through several phases before it is over. How you engage during each phase has an impact on future tantrums and, depending on the temperament of your child, your engagement may even stop them altogether.

If you sense that a tantrum is about to begin and you are unable to prevent it by empathizing, redirecting, or fulfilling the need, first make sure that your child is in a safe place without direct access to potentially dangerous objects. Do not attempt to reason with your child or give in if her demands are unreasonable. Prepare yourself to follow through until the end.

Most tantrums begin with a small wind-up of frustration, followed by an outburst of yelling, screaming, or breath-holding before the child becomes physically aggressive. She might throw toys, shove or pull larger objects like chairs, hit, or kick. The important thing to remember is that children are not able to be reasonable during the height of their emotional outburst. If your child's personality allows her to respond positively to your open arms at this stage, by all means, give her a hug!

However, for most children, giving a lot of verbal or physical attention or attempting to offer solutions during this stage will *lengthen* the tantrum. By staying close by, yet also silent, you are showing your love and respect while you wait for your child to reach a more receptive state of mind. You don't want to ignore your child and walk away, but you don't want to pay too much attention either! Just wait patiently. Let the emotional storm pass. The sun will come out again.

When the yelling and physical aggression subside, you might see your child visibly relax but still continue to cry. The worst is usually over at this point, and you may inch closer, offering physical contact like gently patting her back or pulling her into your lap. Throwing a tantrum is *no* fun. In fact, it hurts. She will be able to hear your words now, so empathize. Tell her that you understand and that you love her. Ask her if she is ready to find a solution with you. Make a suggestion or offer a limited choice.

If you consistently respond to your child by using this method, she will learn that throwing a big tantrum is unnecessary. The outbursts will diminish in intensity as she realizes that she can take a shortcut from that first nagging feeling of frustration right to the outcome: the comfort and safety of being in your loving arms.

Sleeping

If your child hasn't yet made the transition out of a crib, you may want to consider making the shift sometime this year. Most 2-year-olds tend to be risk-takers when it comes to climbing, and if your child is scrambling to get in or out of bed himself, this is a sign that he needs more independence in this area. As with all big routine changes, pick a day to make this shift when your toddler is happy, healthy, and well-rested. In addition, transitions will always be easier if your child is not going through other stressful life events, such as a new potty-learning adventure or the birth of a sibling.

Setting Up the Bed

There are several nice "big kid" bed options to choose from. Your child's crib may already convert into a toddler bed, which are generally low to the ground and fit your child's crib mattress. A bed this size and shape may last your child for a couple more years.

Another option is setting a twin or full mattress directly on the ground or on a low bed frame. If the bed is low to the ground, you don't have to worry about your child falling off. If you choose to go with a regular-size bed and frame, make sure to install side rails (which prevent your child from rolling off) and use a soft rug underneath for any midnight landings. Do not use a bunk bed, as it is not safe for children under the age of 6.

Making the Change

After you have decided on the type of bed, have a conversation with your child to explore his feelings. Tell him that you are excited that he is growing up, and it is time to take down the crib. If he reacts with skepticism, you might place the new bed in exactly the same spot as his old crib and emphasize that it will be just as cozy. You could even keep the crib in the room for a few weeks as he gets used to snuggling in his new bed. If, on the other hand, he reacts with enthusiasm, involve him as much as possible in the new setup. He may want to choose a stuffed animal to place on top and help fluff his covers. Let him have some alone playtime, too. A new bed is like a new toy!

Either way, spend some time cuddling or reading a story in the new bed. Role-play tucking your child into it during the daytime, too, well before bedtime, so that he has time to practice. Remember that transitions often take time, so allow several weeks of consistent reassurance and repetition before you expect your child to feel comfortable in the new routine.

Childcare

Deciding when or whether to place your child into the care of another adult is an extremely personal decision. If you are able and eager to stay at home with your 2-year-old full time, there is no need to enroll her into a daycare or school. However, many parents do need or want to work full time or part time. Fortunately, young children can thrive in either environment as long as it involves a loving relationship with a respectful adult, ample time for playing indoors and outside, and community-based experiences.

Respectful Communication

All relationships require work on both ends, and this truism applies to your interactions with the caregiver or school staff. Nurturing that relationship will be extremely beneficial to your child. If he comes home from daycare unhappy, it is up to you to address the issue. You must be his advocate. To do so effectively, you need to also have an appreciative, respectful attitude toward the caregiver. Start any difficult conversation off with the sentence-starters, "Thank you for . . . " or "I appreciate . . . " This will help get you into the right mind-set and will also put everyone at ease.

Next, express your feelings and describe the problem. Try the phrases, "I am concerned about . . . " or "I was wondering if . . . " Listen with an open mind as your caregiver responds with her point of view. If she understands that you are willing to help, the problem-solving will be much easier. Remember that even though you cannot control everything that happens while you are not present, you are still the parent, and you know what's best for your own child. If the caregiver is using a harsh or manipulative discipline technique that you feel is exacerbating the problem or harming the emotional well-being of your child, you have the right to question it and request that a more developmentally appropriate technique be used. If you are unable to come to a consensus, it is time to find a different caregiver.

Addressing Behavioral Issues

As much as you wish you could ensure that your child is behaving appropriately when not under your supervision, you simply do not have that power. You may feel angry or frustrated if you hear that she has been biting, hitting, or refusing to cooperate. Punishing her at home will not stop the behavioral problem. Instead, you need to have a full understanding of the details, so reach out and communicate respectfully to the caregiver before you take any other action. You need to know exactly when the incident occurred, what happened just before, who else was involved, and how often it is happening. Is it a one-time little situation or a major recurring issue? If it's the latter, ask if there is a way you can observe her behavior in a place where she can't see you watching. Based on all of that information, there are things you can do to help the situation. Remember, even though you are not there during the day, you are not helpless.

Talk to your child. Find out her version of the story. Empathize and connect emotionally. She needs to feel that you are on her side, even if she did make a poor choice.

Involve your child in making a plan. For example, "The next time Sonja tries to take away the toy, go tell the caregiver that you need help instead of hitting Sonja." Role-play to help her commit the words and actions to memory.

Inform the caregiver of the plan in writing. Whether it's a text, email, or handwritten document, write down both the incident and your plan. It will help both of you remember what you've tried in case of future problems.

Prepare at drop-off. Before dropping her off at daycare, remind your child of the plan the two of you agreed upon. She also needs to know that the caregiver is aware of this plan.

Follow up afterward. When you pick your child up from daycare, ask her if she was able to implement the plan. Connect with the caregiver as well and let him know that he has your support.

Continues on page 70

In-Depth Look:
Consistency in Caregiving

You may experience strong emotions when transitioning your child into a new caregiving situation. Many parents feel a mixture of excitement, fear, guilt, and hope. If this describes your current predicament, know that these feelings are all normal and the intensity is likely to subside after you have settled your child into a new, consistent routine. Take the time to consider all of your options for part-time or full-time care. Thoroughly interview any potential babysitters, au pairs, nannies, or other caregivers who will come to your own home. You want to choose someone who is well aligned with your approach to discipline. Take tours of home-based daycares, childcare centers, and preschools and compare the environments they offer. Use the checklists below to guide you in your search.

Potential Caregiver:

· Seems warm, friendly, and nurturing

· Demonstrates an easy rapport with children, such as giving eye contact and speaking respectfully

· Holds certifications and/or has experience in childcare or early childhood education

· Is willing to listen to your parenting philosophy

- Shows interest in your child's personality, including any quirks
- Does not use bribes, threats, spanking, or other coercive methods to gain compliance

Potential Daycare or School:

- The grounds are safe and secure.
- Parents are made to feel welcome when visiting.
- Learning to use the potty is encouraged and supported by the staff.
- Children look joyful and focused on their play or in their interactions with adults.
- Staff members also look joyful and focused on the children.
- Adult:child ratio is fairly low (know the legal requirements in your area).
- Curriculum involves time for play, leaning more heavily on unstructured "free play" time both indoors and outdoors.
- There is a clear policy for informing and involving parents when behavioral issues arise.
- The discipline techniques used by the staff match your own philosophy fairly closely.
- The environment feels "home-like" and is a place where you feel your child would be comfortable.

Continued from page 67

> **Quick Tip:** When your child is learning to use the potty, it will be particularly important that you and your child's caregiver are on the same page about how to handle accidents. Make sure that you have a conversation first if you plan to send him to his caregiver in underwear for the first time.

Non-Compliance

The idea that you can control your child's behavior or shape her future personality is a myth. At this stage, 2-year-olds lack the cognitive development to understand all of the possible consequences of their actions, so our role is to step in with our rational, logical prefrontal cortexes to keep them safe and teach them how to respectfully engage with their world. Being clear with ourselves about our parenting roles (to provide opportunities for learning and protect from harm) and their learning roles (to challenge authority and find things to play with) will help us stay centered when our children push our buttons with impulsive, non-compliant behavior.

Fearless Exploration

Some of the activities your 2-year-old insists on doing may make you feel uncomfortable. He doesn't just want to be up at counter height with you; he also wants to cut with your sharpest knives. He isn't happy playing at ground level; he wants to be way up high on the playground equipment with the big kids. Because he is so much more capable than he was a year ago, and because he has the intense drive to become independent, he may insist on doing things that you know he is not ready for. Here are a few common risk-taking behaviors that toddlers engage in and easy solutions to avoid a struggle.

Coveting your knives: Say "Yes." He's ready for this experience—just not your large chef's knife. Give him a "wavy chopper," a cutting tool often used for slicing vegetables, or a nylon salad knife instead. While you are preparing a meal, he will be able to help with the slicing and dicing. Don't forget to give him his own cutting board and serving bowls, too. Keep these supplies down low where he can reach them.

Climbing up the counters: A nice, sturdy stepstool or a "learning tower," a piece of furniture especially created for toddlers to reach counter height, will help him feel included in the kitchen activities. Also, make sure he has enough opportunities to practice climbing. Playground structures are wonderful for this, but if he can't climb up there by himself, he might not be as safe as you hope. Help support and guide his steps as he works his way up.

Turning the range/oven knobs on: Someday, he will be ready to use the stove or oven alone, but you cannot say "Yes" to this activity at this age. You will need to consistently supervise your child closely in the kitchen and follow through by redirecting him to another activity or removing him from the kitchen altogether if he tests this boundary.

Jumping off high surfaces: You know that five steps up is too high and too far for him to jump to the ground, but he doesn't make that distinction himself—he just wants to try it! You can let him jump with your assistance and close presence if you feel that the risk is low enough. Otherwise scour the jumping area for possible dangers and make a firm, non-negotiable rule about where it is and is not safe to jump. Stay in the area to supervise and enforce your guideline. For a toddler who loves to jump and tumble, create an obstacle course in your living room for him to jump off, crawl under, and scramble over. The more he practices jumping safely from lower heights, the more accurately he will be able to judge for himself what is safe.

When Your Child Says "No!"

This short word may start with a whine and become a wail; the resulting sound is often a reflection of our all-too-human feelings. Your 2-year-old will probably use the word *no* a lot. When distraction and redirection fail to do the job, you are likely to hear "No" over and over—and louder and louder—as your child's protests become more persistent. As you work to regulate your own emotions, which might be bordering on anxiety or anger, try to keep in mind that your child has the right to express her dislike for events or activities imposed upon her, and she also has the right to protest them. If your child never learned how to say no to anything, you'd be worried about her for the rest of her life. Give her simple choices that involve *yes* or *no* questions so that she can practice using the word *no* to express her preferences.

When you find yourself in a battle of wills and there's a complete refusal to cooperate:

Do:	Don't:
☑ Decide quickly what is and is not allowed.	☒ Let the situation drag on and on.
☑ Offer an alternative if possible.	☒ Use sarcasm or laugh.
☑ Physically remove your child or the offending item.	☒ Try to reason or negotiate.
	☒ Ignore your child's feelings.
☑ Empathize with your child's feelings.	☒ Allow your own emotions to get out of control.
☑ Be prepared for a tantrum.	

Afterward, take the time to reflect. Your child dislikes something enough to use a power word over and over. Why? What's bothering her in particular? Is there anything you can change about the environment to prevent her frustration next time?

Containing the Messes

Open cabinets beg to be explored, and too many toys are impossible to put away. Make it easier for your child to play by carefully assessing what is available and within her reach at any given time. At this age, she will be capable of putting her own toys away if there are not too many and she knows exactly where they go. Model taking a toy off of the shelf, playing with it briefly, and then returning it where it goes. If you do this often enough, she will copy your behavior.

However, don't assume that just because she can clean up on her own, she will want to every time. Save those cleanup battles for when she's older and more willing to listen to reason. For now, entice her into cooperation by saying, "Let's clean up together." Sing or dance your way around the room as you put everything back in order. When you're finished, take some time to look around and smile about how nice it all looks.

Toddlers excel at dumping, destroying, and spilling. Water from the bathroom sink, yogurt on her snack table, cornflakes on the floor . . . these everyday spills are going to happen no matter how careful she tries to be, so it's better to be prepared for easy cleanup rather than trying to prevent it altogether. Create a cleanup station with child-size cleaning tools, such as a broom, mop, dustpan, drying cloth, sponge, and spray bottle of water. Be matter-of-fact and calm when the mess happens. Redirect her toward the use of these tools. To her, this is just another fun way to play.

Toileting

Learning to use the potty can be pure joy for a toddler working on this new skill without the overt pressure of adult expectations. In fact, when we think of this process as a learning opportunity instead of a "training" event, we realize that it is the child's responsibility, not ours, to take this big leap toward adulthood. This is not something we are doing to our children. This is something we are helping them learn to do for themselves.

Our job is to provide opportunities for practice and guide with enthusiasm. No bribes or threats are necessary. If you let your child lead the way, you can relax in the knowledge that somehow, sometime, he will use the toilet with confidence.

Parent to Parent:
A Grand Mess

"We love to cook together, so we kept the baking ingredients in a low drawer. My son had been quiet for a while when we heard a giggle from the kitchen. He had taken an almost brand new bag of cornmeal and dumped it EVERYWHERE! He squished his little fingers in it, and basked in the sensation of the cornmeal on his foot. He was clearly so impressed with the grandeur of the mess. All I could think was, "This cornmeal is going to be in the cracks of our floor forever!" But I then reminded myself: It's just cornmeal, and I was the one who made it available.

"Since he was enjoying the feeling of the cornmeal, we used our hands to collect it into a pile. We got dustpans and worked on sweeping up, and then used a damp cloth to wipe the floor. As we cleaned, we talked about saving the ingredients so we would have enough the next time he wanted to bake. I came through later and did a more thorough clean. We still keep ingredients in a low drawer—just less of each one."

— *Kari, 32, from Madison,*
Ohio, parent of two children
(ages 3 years and 5 months)

Signs of Interest

For most children, a burst of interest and ability in toileting can be seen sometime in this second year. You'll recognize it because he can get dressed and undressed with some help; he can also sense when he needs to pee or poop and hold it until he gets to a special place. You may notice him squatting in a hidden place while pooping in his diaper or taking off his diaper altogether to pee uninhibited. He might take a special interest in exploring his private parts and asking about yours. He may become fascinated with the color, size, shape, and texture of his poop.

Be skeptical of any advice that promises full completion of the process on a specific timeline or in a short number of days. Accidents and regressions are common for all children.

Steps for Success

Breaking a habit is hard to do. Your child's everyday diaper routine may have been comforting, bringing feelings of safety and security. He may have even looked forward to the time you spent together bonding during this repetitive and loving ritual. Now, you are changing both expectations and the physical feeling. The absence of that soft, protective barrier on his bottom and the knowledge that he will have to relieve himself elsewhere may make him feel a little anxious, leading to constipation or the outright refusal to cooperate.

It is important that you begin this process with the understanding that learning to use the potty is his job, not yours, but you can make the transition easier by guiding him along the way.

Commit to success and pick a day to start. If you are feeling stressed or anxious about this whole potty thing, it may help to consider whether *you* are ready for your child to make this transition. If you work during the week, Saturday morning is a good time to start. Make sure that your child is healthy, in a good mood, and *not* in the middle of a major life event, such as immediately after the arrival of a new baby sibling or on the day a parent is leaving to go on a business trip. Your confidence and good timing are essential for success.

Put the diapers away. Tell your child that the diapers are not needed anymore during the day. It's time to pee and poop in the potty. If your child does not seem to care, put them away altogether so that they cannot be seen. If your child is more emotionally sensitive and possessive of his beloved diapers, you might find a special place to put them. Note that many children do still need diapers during naptime or at night for several years.

Make the potty accessible. Small, portable potties that are low to the ground are much easier to squat on and a lot less intimidating for toddlers who are just learning. You may keep the little potty in the bathroom or add one to other rooms so that one is always available. Many products are also available for modifying an adult-size toilet with a child-size seat. Don't forget to add a stepstool or small potty ladder made for this purpose.

Go naked on the bottom. For the first few days, at home and in temperate weather, dress your child in a long dress or T-shirt so that there are no clothing obstacles in the way. The next step is wearing pants without underwear. When you have had regular success with this (give it a few weeks), transition to underwear or lightweight cloth training pants.

Don't make a big deal out of it. Learning to use the potty is a normal, natural skill, just like learning to catch a ball. It just requires practice. There's no need to do anything special or different. Leave the treats, screen time, and stickers out of it. In fact, since being naked on the bottom is unusual, it will likely be more comforting to your child to just go about the day normally otherwise.

Hydrate. Don't forget that he needs to drink in order to pee. A glass of water or a serving or two of fruit along with his regular snacks and meals will do.

Observe. Many children will make a "poop face" or do a "pee pee dance" when they feel the urge to go. Watch closely so that you can learn to recognize the subtle signs and get your toddler to the potty as quickly as possible.

Go to the toilet together regularly. If you feel comfortable with the lack of privacy, modeling where pee and poop are "supposed to go" is helpful for children. When he sees you use the toilet, you can mention how he gets to use his little potty now.

Refusal to Cooperate
Did you just tell your toddler it's time to go potty and she yelled, "No!" and ran in the opposite direction? This is typical, so don't get discouraged.

First, random potty reminders can be extremely unwelcome. Toddlers thrive on routines and clear expectations. Find a potty rhythm. Take her to the potty first thing in the morning. Then, look at the rest of your daily routine and think about times when going to the potty would be a natural transition before and after every major activity. For example, you would take her to the potty before eating and after cleaning up the meal, before you leave the house and after you get back, before taking a nap and after waking up, and so on. In between these times, you will be observing and taking her when your gut says it's probably about time. For some children, it may be about 20 minutes after drinking a glass of water. For others, it may be longer. You will need to get to know your child's rhythm and make it part of the routine.

Next, make sure you're clear with your child: potty time is non-negotiable. Chances are good that she will not be able to communicate to you that she needs to go for quite some time, so it is up to you to insist that it is time to go and physically take her there. Be quick, decisive, and enthusiastic. Say, "It's time to go pee," and off you go.

Finally, being asked to go to the potty can feel like an impromptu show for an audience, and all the pre-performance jitters can overwhelm a small child. The answer? Take the pressure off and make potty time fun and relaxing. To a child, all playtime is learning time. If potty time doesn't involve any play, there's no enticement to learn this new skill. Carry your little meowing kitty to the potty one time and ask her if she'd like to be a doggie the next. Read a story or leave a little basket of board books so she can read herself one. (Skip the screen time, as it is more distracting than helpful.) Stay with her and sing songs, make silly sounds, or just talk about your day. When she begins to pee or poop, encourage her to listen to the sound. She may also want to inspect the contents before flushing it away. There is no need to praise or offer a reward, but big accomplishments sometimes call for shared celebrations. Join her by clapping your hands or doing a little happy dance, saying, "You did it!"

Handling Accidents

Do you remember how your child learned to walk? He probably took a few steps and then fell flat on his little bum. He may have cried or giggled in surprise. With your encouragement and support, he learned how to put one foot in front of the other and balance on his own two feet. Learning to use the potty is the same.

For the next year or so, your child might understand that that pee belongs in the potty, but may not be able to recognize that it's coming in time and remember what to do. Or he might be focusing on his play and not want to interrupt his concentration to go take care of the need to pee. Accidents are also common when out and about or on long road trips. Plan ahead by taking a little potty with you in the car and saving time for extra pit stops. If you are at your wit's end and feel like you simply cannot deal with the constant accidents, it is also perfectly okay to put a diaper back on for a few weeks or even a few months and try again from the beginning when you're ready.

Use Your Words: If he wets his clothes or pees on the floor, stay calm and use descriptive words such as, "I see that your pants are wet." Take him directly to the potty area where he may take off his clothes and sit down on the potty to see if there is "any more pee ready to come out." When he is re-dressed in clean clothes, remind him firmly, "Pee goes in the potty." Work together to clean up any messes on the floor and move on to the next activity. Accidents are common through the early childhood years.

CHAPTER
FOUR

3-Year-Olds

At age 3, your child is entering a new period of consciousness. Her mind, while still absorbing all of the sensory experiences of the present moment, is also beginning to understand the concept of past and future. All of her activities have suddenly become more purposeful. She craves choices, a sign that she has grown up and sees herself as capable.

She is no longer beholden to her instinctive needs but is an active participant in her own learning and in her relationships with others. This will be a turning point for your relationship, as the discipline strategies that worked well during the past three years suddenly may no longer fly. It will take both imagination and flexibility to meet the needs of your 3-year-old.

Development

Silly and sweet, your 3-year-old may make you laugh with his goofy antics and zest for daily life. The practical activities that were so difficult to physically manage at age 2, such as washing hands or serving a snack, hold great interest at this age. The joy of messy play continues, but if you can direct his attention toward tiny details, such as that last spot of dirt under his fingernail or the errant pea that rolled under the table, he is likely to go after it with vigor, proudly showing off the result of his handiwork.

This is not to say that everything always goes smoothly. Boundaries continue to be tested. Tantrums may be more severe and thrown with more awareness. Stubbornness is also a common characteristic of this age, as your child is now able to anticipate the future and have the willingness to wait longer to see if you will give in to his demands.

The trick to mitigating this negativity is to focus as much as possible on your child's new and amazing abilities and how much you love him. In short, your child does not just want to be your helper at this age; he wants to be *adored*. Be willing to let him act like a baby for just a bit longer. He will want to hear how much you love him and express his love for you over and over. Let that perspective dominate your parenting this year.

What's New?

Your child may show just as much exuberant energy for physical activity, but her purpose has shifted. No longer does she run just for the sake of running or climb with a focus on strength-building. She runs because she sees something to investigate; she climbs in order to get up to the top of a playground structure so that she can slide down. Pedaling a tricycle or going up and down stairs is much easier, allowing her to focus on the excitement of going somewhere.

Getting enough big muscle movement is essential for her development, but just as important is her need to refine her small motor skills. When she pours herself a drink of water, she is able to do so with far less spilling now, and she may be interested in repeating certain activities over and over until she perfects her movements. She may take an interest in painting or drawing, experimenting with quick, decisive strokes, wavy lines, and circles.

While messy play is still fun, her senses are also becoming more refined. As she strengthens her fine motor skills, she is attuned to temperature, weight, length, and height. This is why block and puzzle play often take center stage during this year. She may express a new interest in learning letters and their sounds or numbers and their corresponding piles of objects. These new concepts may be very exciting for a brief period and then seemingly forgotten in favor of other pursuits. The best educational approach for a 3-year-old will always be child-led.

Because she has a budding awareness of the passage of time, regarding herself now as a "big girl," she may become interested in hearing about what she was like when she was younger. Some 3-year-olds suddenly regress in their speech and exclusively use baby talk for a while. Others pretend to be a baby or a baby animal, such as a kitten or puppy. She may go through phases where she is much more attached to you and refuses to do anything for herself or by herself. These behaviors are common for all children at this age, but may be triggered by the birth of a new sibling.

Becoming aware of your own growth can be scary. This is also the age when new, persistent fears emerge, such as being afraid of the dark, monsters, or barking dogs. Because of this, 3-year-olds need constant reassurance and predictable routines to feel secure. Anxieties are often revealed by a refusal to cooperate during everyday activities or by excessive hyperactivity (usually just before bedtime). Your child is still not grounded in reality and may mix up fantasy with real life.

Playtime in social situations changes dramatically this year. No longer does she sit next to a friend and engage only in her own activity. The two friends are much more likely to participate in a form of cooperative play. They may make up games, take turns with equipment, and play "house" together by re-enacting the roles they see in their social lives. Squabbles are also common and easily solved with a little adult intervention.

Capabilities and Limitations

Puts belongings away: Your child is very sensitive to order at this age, making him particularly aware of whether something is put away in the wrong place. If your child does not have too many toys available at one time and knows exactly where each one belongs, he is capable at this age of returning them to their proper places after he has finished playing. A 3-year-old's willingness to do this depends on his mood. He cannot be depended upon to remember to return all of his items; however, he is easily enticed by the spirit of cooperation, and the reinforcement of extremely predictable "first . . . then" routines.

Develops concentration: You will see an increase in your child's ability to focus on one activity for longer periods. All children achieve deep levels of concentration at different rates depending on their personalities. It is not unusual for a child to still be highly distractible and exhibit an abundance of energy at this age. To encourage concentration, try not to interrupt him to ask questions or correct his work if he is working intently on a single activity. Instead, minimize environmental distractions (such as TV or other background noise) and wait for him to finish before attempting to talk to him.

Shares and takes turns: Unlike the younger toddler years, when the concept of "possession" was fierce, it is now perfectly appropriate to request and expect that your child take turns with toys when siblings or friends are playing in the same space. If your child is not comfortable sharing a personal item with a friend, put it away in a special place before the play date and set the expectation that the remaining toys will be available for anyone to use. Your child is likely to engage in spontaneous sharing as a show of affection if it has been modeled for him. Be aware that he does not yet have a clear concept of time. Instead of giving him a number of minutes to play with an item before returning it, give him a more concrete transition, such as, "After we eat lunch, it will be your sister's turn."

Can be somewhat reasonable: The impulsive nature of the 2-year-old fades as your child gains more self-control and patience. If you tell him not to touch a dangerous object in a serious voice because he will get hurt, he is more likely to pay attention and understand. You can't count on his compliance, however—even in the face of danger. He still needs heavy supervision at this age.

Is more capable of self-care: From brushing his teeth to getting dressed, your child can do so much for himself. This does not mean he will always want to. In fact, 3-year-olds often rebel against their own independent abilities and demand that a parent step in to do things for them. This is your child's way of saying, "I'm still little. I still need you." For now, the best thing to do is to give in and help when he asks, then offer an extra hug or cuddle to make him feel secure and loved.

Use Your Words: Instead of telling your child what to do, try a phrase that indicates cooperation and then describes your next activity together, such as, "Let's put the toys away, and then we can go outside."

Communication

Many 3-year-olds can speak well enough to be understood by others and communicate their needs, which makes life a lot less challenging in some ways. Your child is able to listen to your brief instructions and follow through when motivated to do so. Lecturing will not be effective, so get to the point right away. Use her name to cue her in to your voice, and lean in low, giving lots of eye contact just as you did when she was younger.

Whispering closer to her ear is another great technique you can try if she is having difficulty focusing. Distractibility is still an issue at this age, and you may need to repeat your directions several times. To make sure that she understands what she is supposed to do, ask her to repeat the directions back to you so that you know for sure she understands.

Age-Appropriate Discipline

Instead of expecting your 3-year-old to obey your every command, empower him with meaningful choices. As the responsible adult, there will be many times when you need to make a decision and follow through. Your child is still depending on you to be that secure base as he explores. However, helping him tap into his developing compassion for others will benefit all of you so much more than his mere compliance with your rules.

He no longer only reacts to the immediate moment; he is beginning to mentally prepare himself for what will come next. Self-reflection is one of his biggest new developmental shifts this year. His mind is moving quickly past the *what* and is searching constantly for the *why, when, how,* and *where*. He will want you to teach him so much about the world, including how to respect himself, others, and the environment.

Provide Purposeful Work

To get our own adult chores done, we often look to toy collections, hoping that they will keep our children busy—even for a little while. While having unstructured playtime is a wonderful and necessary part of childhood, it is not enough. Because she looks to you as her role model, she is not satisfied with remaining outside of your adult world and will use many attention-getting strategies if she feels isolated. She wants to emulate you and participate in work that serves a real purpose.

Take note of the regular chores you complete on a daily basis, such as washing dishes, laundry, vacuuming, or yard work. Then, think about ways you can involve her in this real, practical life work by practicing the skills she needs to learn to do them independently. Perhaps on a day when she is particularly energetic, you could provide her with a small rake and a yard full of big, dry leaves. When you are doing the laundry, you might give her a pile of her own and show her how to carefully fold a washcloth in half and put it away.

Her busy little working hands will allow her mind to make discoveries about the world, and they also bring her body and spirit into a more peaceful, calm state of being. Offering meaningful work is a discipline strategy that is often overlooked, but if your child appears anxious, overexcited, mischievous, or disgruntled, it is a worthy technique to try.

Give Information

There is so much your child does not know about the world, and he will make many mistakes just like any other human being. To teach him an effective lesson about the world, pick the right teachable moment.

When you stop your child from engaging in a certain behavior, he is more concerned with his own emotions and the fact that you are preventing him from continuing his fun than hearing what you have to say. For example, when he is running across the room with scissors outstretched, you know that it is an unsafe behavior you must put a stop to. You can remind him, "No running with scissors," but he is unlikely to remember this lesson if he is focused on his own purpose, which may be getting quickly to the supply of construction paper. After calmly helping him get what he needs for the project, you need to make a plan for giving him the information he needs about scissors.

Either before he uses the scissors again or after he has completed his current project, sit down briefly with him in a focused way to give the information he needs. He needs to know that scissors are sharp. He needs to know how to hold them correctly and demonstrate to you that he can do so. He needs to know what could happen if he uses them in a dangerous way. This is all information that will help him make an informed choice the next time he wants to use the scissors. As he is only 3 and cannot yet be trusted, you will need to follow up again later with a reminder of your discussion.

Use Your Words: When giving information to your child, you need to find a calm moment when he can listen to you. Then try starting with the words, "There's something you need to know about [subject]."

Use Natural Consequences

Natural consequences are the results of our behaviors and choices. They apply to both you and your child, and being aware of them will help you to evaluate whether you need to pick a battle or whether you can empathize and allow your child to learn from her own mistakes without intervention.

For example, let's say that you told your child that she may have three strawberries every day, and that way the strawberry supply will last all week. You dole out three strawberries and leave the rest of the box in front of her on the counter. After turning your back for just a minute, you are surprised to see her eating the very last strawberry in the box. Your first response may be anger: she defied you! It is important to also consider that she still lacks impulse control and logical reasoning at this young age.

One natural consequence of her actions could include a stomachache, but another more relevant consequence is the simple fact that there will be no more strawberries for her to eat. She won't learn this lesson overnight, but over a longer period. If she asks for more, you can state the truth: They are gone until the next grocery shopping day.

The lesson will certainly be more impactful if you take the time to empathize with her desire to eat all those delicious berries. And the follow-up might be to strengthen your relationship by including her in a plan for next time, such as letting her separate the strawberries into small containers and labeling them. You will also remember the consequences of *your* actions and remember to store the rest of the strawberries immediately next time. Acknowledging these natural consequences is a learning opportunity for both of you.

Use Logical Consequences

Eating an entire box of strawberries, of course, is unlikely to cause much harm to children without allergies. The natural consequences are reasonable. There will be times, however, when the natural consequences are too problematic or dangerous for you to allow them to play out. A child who refuses to wear a coat in cool weather will feel the chill but suffer little, but a child who tries to run around without proper clothing in the snow could face hypothermia and frostbite. This is not reasonable or safe, so you must impose a logical consequence, such as returning indoors together.

Setting your expectations beforehand will help a great deal. The kinds of consequences that are most helpful for children are ones that are fair, reasonable, lead to the development of self-control, and strengthen relationships.

Consider another common situation parents of 3-year-olds face in the grocery store. If your child begins to run wildly around and resists your reminders and other attempts to calm him, you may need to lay out a firm choice: "You can choose to walk and we can keep shopping or you can choose to keep running and we will need to leave the store." If your child chooses to run again, you will need to physically remove him, which is the logical consequence. In this case, there will also be many natural possible consequences of his actions. He may tip over a large display and you will be responsible for the damages. He may cause another shopper to trip and fall, causing both him and the other person to get hurt. You cannot allow these to happen, so a logical consequence it must be.

Remember that it is easy for a logical consequence to be twisted into a punishment. If you find yourself feeling angry and wanting your child to suffer in some way for his misbehavior, this would be a moment to pause and re-evaluate whether the consequence you are considering is fair and just, or if it is actually punitive.

Continues on page 96

In-Depth Look:
Why Punishment Doesn't Work

Consequences are often misinterpreted as punishments; if they are applied in this way, they will not be effective. Punishing a child through spanking, isolation, the withholding of special treats or events, or removal of beloved toys does not teach worthy life lessons. After a punishment, instead of merely thinking it over and deciding to happily comply next time, most children become emotionally stuck in a state of despair, regret, anger, or resentment.

Parents who want to avoid spanking may be tempted to go right to a "time-out" method in which a non-compliant child is taken to a chair, a spot on the floor, or a corner and is not allowed to get up for a certain number of minutes. When time-outs are used frequently, the child may act as though they have no effect at all, laughing or disobeying on purpose. Frustrated parents may be tempted to choose harsher punishments because the time-outs just aren't that effective in the long run.

When parents use these techniques, the message the child receives is this: "If I don't obey, I will be made to suffer." Unfortunately, suffering is a human condition and includes feelings of loneliness, guilt, anxiety, and sadness. We all experience some kind of suffering during the course of our lives when we make mistakes. There is no need to try to make a child feel this way. What we want is to make sure our children stay safe and find an appropriate teaching moment so that learning happens, not suffering.

Instead of: "If you don't stop whining right now, you're getting a spanking."

Try: "I understand how hard it is to have patience while we wait. Waiting is so hard. I know we will both feel so much better when we're home and we can relax and read a story together."

Instead of: "I've had it with your behavior. That's a time-out!"

Try: "I am feeling so frustrated. I need to step away and go calm myself down."

Instead of: "If you won't pick up your toys, I'm throwing them away."

Try: "Let's pick up your toys together, and then we will have a dance party."

As our children's protectors and educators, we must help them learn from their mistakes and guide them toward making choices that lead to the best rewards of all: solid self-esteem and healthy relationships with others.

Continued from page 93
Common Issues

From impatience to anxiety, your 3-year-old still needs your love and guidance. Here are some explorations of the biggest issues parents face this year with tips for making it a smoother ride all around.

Tantrums

Since 2-year-olds are renowned for terrible tantrums, you might expect your 3-year-old to sail through the year. Most 3-year-olds do continue to struggle with emotional outbursts, however. In the previous year, your child had very little control over his behavior, but now he is becoming more self-aware, making a connection between behavior and outcome. Some tantrums at this age may be bids for your attention. This does not make them any less real, but how you evaluate the situation and respond may be a little different. Patience and compassion remain the most essential strategies (see pages 30 and 31), but you will also need to directly teach your child problem-solving skills.

Determining What to Teach

When your child throws a fit, determining the real reason why is the key to helping her find a different way to express her feelings in the future. Acknowledge her feelings and offer comfort, but don't oversympathize. Just as when she was little, wait patiently for the storm to pass, and do not give in to her demands. Now that she is 3, she will be more receptive to your instruction, so think about what life lessons you might impart both immediately afterward and in daily life.

Here are a few common reasons 3-year-olds throw tantrums and suggestions for teaching helpful skills:

Frustration: You said "No" to what she wants. She is just letting you know how disappointed and angry she is and hoping you will change your mind (don't give in!). At another time, teach her the right words to say to express emotions and practice them. You can look at books or pictures of facial expressions and name them together, using a mirror to mimic them. You can give her a one-liner to say when she feels frustration, such as "I'm not happy!" or "I want that."

Delayed gratification: You said "Yes" to what she wanted, but it's not coming fast enough. Tell her that you understand. Teach her how to wait patiently by giving her specific body actions to perform, such as putting her hands in her lap, taking a big breath, and relaxing her body. You may even regularly suggest that she sing a song or read a book to herself as she waits. Children can also be emotionally on edge when a big holiday is coming up, causing more frequent tantrums. Help her by making a visual schedule so that you can count off the days together and do your best to keep any extra stimulation to a minimum.

Attention-seeking: She feels bored or ignored, and she wants your attention. When you don't give it to her right away or in the way she expects, she tries in bigger, louder, and more disruptive ways. First, evaluate whether you are giving her enough of your undivided attention on a daily basis. Screen time and other hobbies can be a heavy distraction from parenting, taking up more time than you realize. When she needs you, make a habit of completely stopping what you are doing and tuning in. Then teach her more appropriate physical ways to get your attention, such as tapping on your shoulder or placing a hand on your upper arm. Practice this method several times so that both of you understand your roles.

Stress-Induced Meltdowns

The noise in a bustling store during the holiday season or a crowded playground may be too much for your 3-year-old to handle. Some children are more sensitive to external stimulation, so be mindful of your child's personal sensory thresholds. Teach him how to go to a calmer space to get away from the noise, or offer a comfort object to ground him when he can't leave. Children with special sensory needs also may benefit from therapeutic interventions, so if meltdowns are predictably explosive and consistently sensory-related, talk to your child's doctor.

If the tantrums have suddenly increased in frequency and duration, it may be a reaction to a stressful experience. For example, you notice that a few weeks ago, tantrums were rare, but recently you changed his nighttime routine from sleeping in your bed to sleeping in his own. It seems successful to you, but it may have raised his overall stress level and reduced his ability to cope. In other words, his cup is full of enough stress already and additional frustrations are causing it to spill over, resulting in meltdowns.

Avoiding stress altogether is not an option. Learning how to face and cope with adversity is a skill your child needs for life. Other common stress-inducing triggers may include a recent major injury, moving, an unemployed parent or a parent who suddenly returns to work, or witnessing his parents argue. Be patient as he works through his emotions. Describe what you see in his behavior and teach him how to verbalize his worries. You might say, "I wonder if you are feeling extra sad because I had to go to work yesterday. I missed you. Do you want to talk about it?" Finally, be flexible so that he isn't taking on so much frustration at once, even if you need to let some minor things slide for a while.

Quick Tip: Although your 3-year-old may start to look more like a small version of an adult, he still lacks the ability to regulate his own emotions. You may notice that your child is able to "hold it together" when at preschool, on a play date, or with a different caregiver, but as soon as he returns home, he is suddenly non-compliant, whiny, and prone to tantrums. This is normal behavior for young children, who often see home as a safe place to let out all the frustrations that were bottled up during the day.

Fears

New fears often arise during unexpected situations and without warning. Your child's new outlook on life may make her realize that she is vulnerable in ways she hadn't considered before. Many parents find these new fears concerning and perhaps exasperating, especially if they appear irrational. Reassure her that she is safe and loved, but don't say "You're okay" if she's acting visibly afraid. Signs of real fear include shaking, lack of eye contact, clutching tightly, or even complaining of a tummy hurting. Some children also express their fears in combative ways. If your child begins acting unusually non-compliant, defiantly hyper, or physically aggressive, fear could very well be the underlying reason.

Reassuring Your Anxious Child

Briefly validate your child's emotional state, and when you speak, do your best to convey a calm, confident tone of voice. Tell her that you understand how she feels and also that you are not at all worried. Most of all, try not to overreact with excessive comforting or force your child to confront the source of the fear. Both of these approaches can prolong the fearful periods. Instead, assume that this is a phase that will soon pass if you are patient.

Giving information about the scary event or object can be extremely helpful. Many children develop fears of loud noises, such as barking dogs, balloons popping, or fireworks. Take some time to explain these in detail. You might find that your child's curiosity outweighs the fear. Dogs bark to say hello and to warn their owners that strangers are approaching. Balloons are full of air under pressure and make a loud sound when the pressure is suddenly released. Fireworks are tubes full of powder that make bright colors in the dark sky when they are touched by fire. We use them for celebrating.

Other common fears you can easily explain include unexpected changes, such as when Daddy shaves off his beard, or a fear of the dark, which has long encouraged humans to stay put at night so they are safe and sound from bumping into objects that can't be seen.

Differentiating Reality from Fantasy

Dog or dragon? Understanding which animal is real and which is a product of human imagination is obvious to adults, but your child is not able to make this distinction. At age 3, his brain assumes that everything he is exposed to is real, including cartoon or fairy tale characters, mythological creatures, and anthropomorphic animals in storybooks. Even if you tell him these are all pretend, in his mind, they will still *feel* equally real to him and therefore, *scary*.

People dressed in costumes may be more disturbing than fun. To one child, the idea of Santa Claus descending down a chimney is hilarious; to another, it is just as frightening as a burglar. This means that when we expose our children to literature and other forms of media, such as shows or movies, we must be sensitive to this developmental stage. Take the time to ground your child in reality by affirming over and over what is real and what is pretend. If he is afraid, put the book away to allow him time to mature. Focus instead on stories about children overcoming adversity in small, nonthreatening ways.

As they get older, children do benefit emotionally from the role-playing opportunities in common folk or fairy tales. There are many folk tales accessible to children that involve an unlikely hero outwitting a more powerful character. When using a fairy tale or folk tale at this tender age, you must be careful to emphasize what is real and what is fantasy because children are not able to make the distinction themselves. Keep the stories simple and make sure that the moral of the story is an empowering one. Note that some children will reject these adventure tales completely, and others will thrive on the drama and beg for more. Know your child and his limits.

> **Quick Tip:** Holidays and events that involve costumes, such as trick-or-treating on Halloween or sitting on Santa's lap, might be stressful for your young child. Give lots of information about these events before they happen so that your child knows what to expect—and if he's scared, be prepared to let it go. He might simply need another year or two before he enjoys the experience.

Managing Screen Time

How much screen time is appropriate and at what age? Certainly videochatting relatives or friends who live far away seems like a healthy use of screen time for children of all ages. Many parents allow their 3-year-olds to watch a limited number of educational shows or use tablets to play simple games. Some choose to avoid these types of media altogether. Whether your child is exposed to this form of technology, and how often, is a personal decision you will need to make based on your family's needs and careful observation of your own child's behavior.

A Common Battleground

Screen-based technologies are evolving at an incredible rate. The biology of our children's brains, however, takes many generations to fully adapt to new stimuli in our environment. This knowledge alone gives many child development experts pause.

Parents often note that after watching a more violent or fast-paced show, their children tend to act more aggressively and show a lack of focus in their playtime. In contrast, after watching a slower-paced educational show, their children tend to exhibit more peaceful, prosocial behaviors. Parent involvement seems to have a big impact on the overall educational experience as well. When a parent watches a show and pauses it regularly in order to give insight and interpret the actions of the characters, these little breaks allow time for the child to process the story and ask questions.

Too much time spent in front of a screen prevents children from practicing other important skills, such as gross and fine motor skills and imaginative play. Children at this age still learn best through hands-on, sensory-rich activities, which cannot be replicated by the passive viewing experience of watching a show or even the finger-swiping of an app. In addition, if screens are used before bedtime, they can also interfere with a child's ability to fall asleep and stay asleep.

Children may resist turning off the screen, showing signs of distress or throwing full-on tantrums when it's time to transition to a different activity. If your child is constantly arguing with you over the use of your phone, tablet, TV, or other forms of screen-based media, it's time to make a change. You need a family media plan.

Your Family Media Plan

Unless your policy is to go entirely screen-free, it is helpful to have a plan in place for how to handle screen-based media in your household.

1. Decide what screen-based media is allowable.

2. Set age-appropriate time limits. (Consider 1 hour a day.)

3. Make sure that all adults in the family understand and agree to the plan.

4. Remind your child of the expectations before screen-based media is offered.

5. Be aware of the time.

6. Give a warning that screen time is going to end soon.

7. Stay firm and don't give in to more screen time if there is begging.

The media plan you start with may not be reasonable a year or two later, so feel free to re-evaluate your plan periodically. In addition, many parents do make exceptions for special occasions such as holidays or road trips with few ill effects. When you return to your normal routine, a one- or two-week break from screen time will help to reset everyone's expectations.

Social Relationships

Healthy relationships with other people take time to cultivate. By modeling polite behavior, you are teaching your child that communicating respect is a firm expectation in all social interactions.

Managing Conflict

True cooperative play begins this year as your child experiments with turn-taking and resolving conflicts. She might not be good at this at first; it is not uncommon to see children act aggressively toward one another. If two children are physically fighting, it is your first job to separate their bodies so that they cannot inflict any more harm. You will then need to act as a mediator, acknowledging hurt feelings. If the children are unable to verbalize their own feelings, do it on their behalf. For example, "Margaret is feeling upset because she was not done playing with this toy. Carter is feeling confused because he thought this toy was available to play with." Follow this by offering a clear and reasonable suggestion, such as agreeing on a time for turn-taking or suggesting a cooperative play solution. Designating an area for each person, such as a table or individual-size rug, may help some children feel more secure and supported.

Unless there is physical aggression, be wary of stepping in to mediate too often. Stay close by and observe for a little while before intervening. Sometimes children can solve their problems in creative ways all on their own. Afterward, you might draw their attention to it and verbally admire their problem-solving. For example, say, "I noticed that the two of you were upset with each other on the playground, but you figured out a solution that worked for both of you! I'm so glad that you know how to be good friends."

Use Your Words: An apology can be a powerful way to mend hurt feelings, but it should never be forced. True regret comes from the heart. Instead of the common authoritarian demand to "Say you're sorry," try a more open-ended approach, such as, "Neha's feelings were hurt. What can we do to make her feel better?" Your child might then verbally apologize, but she also may offer a hug or a handshake, and those are also valid and respectful.

Preparing for a New Sibling

The addition of a new member of the family is a major life event for a child. He may respond to the stress with feigned indifference, defiance, clinginess, or behavioral regressions. If he is fully capable of wearing underwear and using the toilet, he may begin having accidents again. He may begin to use baby talk or want to sleep in your bed again. These behaviors will all resolve themselves in time, but don't be surprised if it takes a few months.

Although you may not be able to prevent all of the stress, you can work right from the beginning to set your child up for a smoother transition. Start by examining your current routine. Is it working well? Will it need to change when the baby is born? If so, how? Consider making any major changes to your older child's daily outings or bedtime well in advance of your baby's birth so that your older child can rely on that consistency.

Reading books about pregnancy and birth or the adoption process and caring for a newborn or a newly adopted child can give your older child an idea of what to expect. The time you spend together reading also gives him the opportunity to ask questions and allows you to clear up any confusion and calm fears. Many children express interest in the topic of how babies are made. Answer your child's questions honestly, but keep the information simplistic and fact-based. This is actually a wonderful time to have that first discussion about reproduction, as 3-year-olds are old enough to begin conceptualizing basic human biology but young enough to not feel embarrassed by it.

Once the new baby comes, involve your older child as much as possible. There will be times, such as during feeding or diapering sessions, when you will need to give your full attention to the new baby. Talk about this issue with your older child and have him select and set aside some special toys or books to keep close to the rocking chair or changing table.

Many parents also purchase a baby doll that can be dressed and a mini baby doll carrier or stroller so that your older child can role-play the activities you're doing with your real baby. Your child may also enjoy participating in the baby care. Keep a few diapers down low so that he can be your helper and retrieve them for you.

He may also enjoy a new big brother role as the court jester, entertaining your baby during those longer diaper changes and car rides.

Finally, regularly set aside some uninterrupted time to spend alone with your older child. Whether you just sit and read a story, cuddle before bedtime, or share a moment or two coloring with crayons, he will appreciate the extra attention, and it will help to soothe those feelings of jealousy.

Non-Compliance

Her body stiffens, fists clench, chest puffs, chin rises. Her pose says it all: defiance. No longer easily distractible, your 3-year-old has learned how to say "No" and mean it. So, now it's your move. What will you do?

It's still important to remember that even at this age, when your child is more aware of her own choices, saying "Yes" if at all possible and picking your battles carefully will make everything go more smoothly in the long run. The big difference now is that your child is much more receptive to being taught direct lessons about appropriate behavior. Take the time to thoroughly prepare your child for any new event, model the behavior you'd like to see, and give your child some autonomy over her choices.

Going Out in Public

Witnessing your child's inappropriate social behavior in public can be embarrassing. Many parents find themselves either reacting overly harshly or caving in completely to avoid public meltdowns that happen outside of the predictable home environment. While completely understandable, neither approach is good for the child.

Outings can be educational opportunities. Head off non-compliance by scheduling your outing when your child is well-rested and recently fed. Before you go, remind your child of your expectations, such as walking instead of running indoors, sitting quietly, sticking to the shopping list, or saying thank you to the person who helps you. Anticipate possible issues and role-play what you will do if a scenario doesn't go the way she expects. For example, "What will you do if Aunt Mei offers you some food you do not want to eat?" Teach your child how to say, "No, thank you" before you even get to her house. Before visiting the dentist or doctor, it's always a good idea to discuss in detail what you think might happen and let her vent her worries at home if she has any.

While you are out, involve your child in the process as much as possible. Allow her to count the fruit, put items in the cart, and make little decisions along the way. When she gets antsy, offer a snack, play "I spy," tell a story, or pretend to be an animal. If other adults seem to be annoyed or are rude, apologize if necessary, but don't be afraid to speak up on behalf of your child. Children are members of the community who also deserve the right to be themselves in public. If your child's behavior is clearly unacceptable, remind your child of the natural or logical consequence: "If we cannot wait patiently in line to mail this letter, we will need to leave the post office because we are bothering the other customers." If the behavior continues, you must follow through with the consequence, even if it means going outside for a little while. Sometimes discipline is inconvenient for us as parents. Fortunately, your child will quickly learn what is and is not acceptable in public.

After the outing, summarize what worked, what didn't, and what you will try to do next time to avoid any unpleasantness. What lessons might your child benefit from in the future? Consider the following and practice these or other relevant skills in preparation of the next outing. Does your child know how to:

- greet someone new?
- open a door for someone?
- walk next to a shopping cart?
- select an item from a shelf and put it in a basket?
- sit on a couch and have a formal conversation?
- answer *yes* or *no* questions politely?
- wait patiently for her turn?

Insisting on Independence

Your child's insistence on doing things his way continues to be an issue. He may see himself as so capable that he neglects to ask you for permission to do things that are a bit beyond his actual ability level. If you regularly allow him to help in the kitchen, for example, you might find him up on top of your counter one day dumping out the flour to make himself a cake. Or you might walk into the living room to find the floor covered in bath towels next to an empty milk gallon because, "I spilled my milk but cleaned it up, Daddy!"

If your little mischief-maker creates a big mess, take a deep breath and remember that these exasperating times won't last forever. If your child is trying to do things that are a bit too difficult for him, think about ways that you can make them accessible. Can you put a reasonable amount of milk in a small pitcher for him to pour more easily? How about adding a stool so that he doesn't need to climb the counter? You can also set boundaries here, such as, "You may get out the measuring cups to make a cake, but you need to ask first before you get out the flour."

Resisting Independence

Just as strong as your child's need to be independent is his need to remain your little baby. He may refuse to get dressed or paint his own artwork. When you ask him to go get in his bed, he may insist that you carry him there. Some 3-year-olds will even act like their idea of a baby by going limp in your arms, refusing to do anything you ask, or hiding shyly behind your legs. Others may behave as they imagine a baby animal would, meowing or barking and nuzzling your legs to be petted. Learning to use the potty may also continue to be a challenge. Many parents sigh and wonder when this independence will ever come when they hear the call, "Mooooooommmmmyyyyyy, wipe my bottom!"

This push and pull between dependence and independence is normal, and yes, your child will someday be the confident, independent little soul you know he can be. Growing up isn't easy. Narrow down what you are asking him to do into smaller steps. If he still resists your little pushes toward independence, he may be trying to tell you that he could use a little more of your affection and reassurance. Set aside some time for extra snuggles and you'll soon find him taking initiative on his own.

Parent to Parent:
When You Lose Control

"I was raised in a very hostile environment. I swore I would never yell at my child, but I do. I try very hard to catch myself before it goes that far and explain that I'm getting very frustrated, but I don't always get the opportunity. So when it happens, my daughter reacts by screaming at the top of her lungs and then starts crying.

"Sometimes I need to walk away, and I tell her I need a time-out to cool down. I do some breathing and usually text my husband. By then, she comes looking for me. We sit down together and talk about our feelings and why I got so mad. We apologize and move on. I think the most important thing is to keep the line of communication open and assure her that it's perfectly normal to have big emotions."

— Gayle, 35, from Kalamazoo,
Michigan, parent of two children
(ages 3 years and a newborn)

CHAPTER
FIVE

4-Year-Olds

The investigative spirit and "can do" attitude of a typical 4-year-old is a welcome change from last year's occasional clinginess. Before you even ask, your child may run off and handle a problem with surprising ingenuity and then come drag you over to see with a proud smile. Although he still craves your attention, he no longer sees himself as a baby but as a proper citizen of his community, ready and able to take care of the whole world if need be. The exit from toddlerhood is full of grand gestures. Lean in and enjoy this wonderful age. This year, your most effective discipline strategies will center on strengthening your relationship.

Development

Responsibility is a defining theme for your child this year. She is now able to work purposefully on tasks and complete them in shorter time frames. Games and stories that involve some element of justice or collaboration resonate strongly with her, as does the concept of what it means to be a friend to others. Many 4-year-olds are constantly asking wh- questions (why, where, who, what, when) and connecting that information to previous knowledge about the world, making learning adventures easy to come by because there is such a strong desire to *know*.

What's New?

By now, your 4-year-old might be skipping, hopping, and jumping over anything in his path, daring himself to climb higher and run farther than ever before. "Watch me, watch me!" he may yell, as he attempts to balance and practice walking back and forth on any straight and narrow path before him. No organized sports are needed for this playful, energetic child—the simple pleasure of catching a ball and throwing it back is motivation enough.

Indoors, he is capable of pouring without much of a spill most of the time. He has developed enough fine motor skills to use a variety of real tools, such as cutting fruit with a small, blunt-tipped knife, pounding nails into wood with a child-size hammer, and snipping paper with a pair of blunt-tipped child-size scissors, although he will still need lots of adult supervision and clear safety precautions with these experiences.

You'll find that 4-year-olds also have the cognitive readiness for some academic explorations, and many will begin to associate letter sounds with letter names and perform basic mathematical operations. There is one big caveat: All education at this age must occur through playful exploration with concrete materials, and the best approach is always child-led. Fortunately, 4-year-olds are incredibly curious and intrinsically motivated. They also are able to communicate well enough to ask questions, predict outcomes, and share their own experiences. To spark the child's interest in learning a new concept, all one needs to do is demonstrate with enthusiasm.

Your child's life should not be centered on academics this year, however. Creative play takes center stage, as all the new information he is taking in must be processed. Unlike a young toddler, whose pretend play typically mimics adult role-modeling, the more mature mind of the 4-year-old spends time dreaming of all the possibilities that could exist, despite evidence to the contrary. Fact and fiction still remain fairly indistinguishable, so it's our job to give him the security of being able to rely on us to tell him the truth and nurture him with real-life experiences. This allows him to let his own imagination take him wherever he wants to go, no matter what dire consequences are involved in his tales, because he knows you are there to keep him safe.

Many 4-year-olds love to be with friends, make new friends, and experiment with a variety of collaborative and competitive play settings. A group of children "playing house" together may suddenly shift into a wild chase of "bad guys" and then just as quickly change into a hospital team operating on a sick patient. Because socializing is so important at this age, a shy or socially awkward child left out of this community playground adventure may feel isolated and need your help with inserting himself into each scene as the children's stories evolve.

Capabilities and Limitations

Friendly and funny, your 4-year-old is solidifying her place in your family structure and your larger community. She can do so much more now than ever before, and she knows it, but she still needs a lot of hands-on guidance.

Is socially aware: Through the eyes of a 4-year-old a friend is a person who plays with you in the immediate moment. Unlike the singular, "best friend" relationships that older children develop based on shared interests, 4-year-olds benefit greatly from regular exposure to a diverse base of peers. Big, cooperative projects and activities give them ample opportunity for problem-solving and resolving personal conflicts. Adult observation and occasional intervention is essential, because in their quest to determine social status among their peers, they also experiment with the ability to control the behavior of others or manipulate a situation. Bullying can be an issue at this age, as well as misinterpreting group dynamics.

Appreciates boundaries: Clear rules regarding appropriate behavior are internalized, not necessarily because the child understands the reasoning behind them, but because those limits provide physical and emotional security. Your 4-year-old will also likely take pride in pointing out any minor infractions of these rules, whether it involves a peer, an unfamiliar adult, or—most amusingly—occasionally you, the creator of the rules. As good as she is at committing these rules to memory, she is unable to transfer them from one situation to another, and any gray areas are especially frustrating. The ability to create self-imposed boundaries and understand the nuances will come later in her development as her brain matures. This places the burden of setting clear expectations on you, as the adult.

Can be somewhat reasonable: Lengthy, complicated explanations still overwhelm and confuse her, but your child is capable of associating actions with consequences and making compromises. Negotiating for what she wants is a skill she needs to practice, so she is looking for opportunities to do so under your protection. Her tendency to focus on fairness will make her a more reasonable and trustworthy partner on your daily adventures together. Be aware that through all her bravado, she is still an impulsive creature, prone to testing those very limits she worked so hard to negotiate. Supervision is essential.

Expresses emotions fairly effectively: Most 4-year-olds develop conversation skills by asking a lot of questions about the world. When she is upset or angry, she will be able to identify her own emotions and express her feelings to others. She also has much more awareness and control over her body language, and can often be seen posturing dramatically in front of the mirror for self-assessments and in front of others to gauge reactions. Communicating kindness is not her entire agenda, however; many 4-year-olds become near-obsessed with profanity and name-calling. At this age, children are learning about the meanings of words in different social contexts, and they learn that words have varying degrees of power. They are looking for the reactions from the people around them to see the impact, and when they swear or use words like "poop," there is often a bigger reaction.

Communication

Children of all ages can tell when you're actually paying attention and when you are responding while distracted. When your child was younger, he may have more easily accepted your half-attention at times, but a typical 4-year-old can be much more demanding. It's not uncommon for him to try to physically turn your head to look or to ramp up obnoxious behaviors or increase his volume until you finally give him your full attention. As always, when explaining rules, routines, or new expectations for behavior, lean down low to your child's level and speak in a calm tone at medium to low volume. A whisper is often heard much better than a yell.

Unless you are talking about a serious topic, don't be afraid to get silly and messy. Your 4-year-old will feel more secure and loved when you share in the laughter and excitement that comes so easily at this age. An overly serious demeanor is likely to be met with defiance, while a playful "wink-wink" attitude will yield you a good deal more cooperation. There is a balance, of course, as too much silliness from the adult can have the opposite effect, amplifying any hyperactive tendencies of the child.

Children often have big worries at this age about social relationships and the concept of death. These conversations are best had either while you are in physical contact, such as while cuddling on the couch, or in the middle of an activity, while little fingers are busy manipulating a toy or preparing food. With the body engaged and grounded, the mind is free to explore emotions and tune into your voice.

As much as they love the idea of rules, 4-year-olds love being included in the decision-making process. By offering choices throughout the day, you are communicating to your child that his opinion matters. He will take great pride in that responsibility. Rather than directing him to an answer, take a more open-ended approach, using suggestions that lead him to a reasonable conclusion, such as "I wonder what would happen if you . . . " or "I'm curious what you think about. . . . " These give him the opportunity to make discoveries, which will leave a much longer-lasting impression on his behavior.

Quick Tip: Making eye contact may be difficult for some children, especially those with a shy, sensitive personality or those who are neurodivergent. Don't assume that your child is not listening just because she is not looking at you. Rather than requiring mutual eye contact, make a habit of being emotionally present and patient when communicating with your child.

Age-Appropriate Discipline

Since your child feels so much more grown up now, using the "distract and redirect" technique no longer works. Your child can be distracted in the moment, but since she now has deeper levels of concentration and a clearer concept of the passage of time, she is not likely to forget her original request and will feel unfairly manipulated. She wants to be taken seriously and share in responsibilities. Most 4-year-olds engage in a variety of new and annoying behaviors, such as whining or using rude words. Ignore the behavior and focus instead on the *reason* she is trying to get your attention in the first place. Gain her cooperation and a better attitude by making her an active participant in finding solutions.

At this stage, 4-year-olds can be persistent when bargaining for a preferred outcome; resist the urge to use rewards or threats. They may make you the "winner" of the argument in the short run, but using them teaches your child that it is acceptable to manipulate the emotions and behavior of others to get your own way. Fortunately, offering choices remains an effective technique at this age, as well as stating the natural or logical consequences, giving descriptive information about the problem, and following through quickly with whatever decision is made. In addition to the strategies that worked well at age 3 (see page 89), your child will now also benefit from techniques that emphasize community norms, along with a good deal more cooperative strategizing.

Create Family Policies

As far as your child is concerned, too much structure without any flexibility invites a rebellious attitude. In contrast, too much freedom feels overwhelming and results in attention-getting behavior. The key to fostering responsibility and emotional security is to find a happy medium. Your family rules must feel reasonable and attainable. Whether or not your child can read yet, writing down the most important expectations in a simple bullet-point or numbered list helps everyone in the family remember them. A child who has participated in the development of a family policy is much more likely to follow it.

Start by calling a meeting with the whole family. State the issue, and then take turns expressing your feelings. Together, come up with a few rules that everyone can agree upon. For example, if your child has just received a new scooter as a gift from a relative, take the time to anticipate any potential problems and set up the ground rules from the get-go. You might say something like, "Lia has a brand new scooter. I wanted to hear from her how she feels about it, and I'd like for us to think about how we can help her enjoy her gift while staying safe." Your family now discusses their feelings on the issues, such as reasons why helmets are important and the safest places for Lia to ride.

At the end of the meeting, you might announce, "Okay, so we have decided on two main rules for scooters in our family. While an adult is outside to supervise, Lia may ride her scooter by herself to the end of the block and back on the sidewalk. She also needs to wear a helmet. Is there anything else we need to discuss?" If everyone, including Lia, is in agreement, it's time to put the rules into action and let her give it a try. After she successfully completes her first scooter ride, thank her for following the rules and express your excitement for her next adventure. It's also a good idea to give a little reminder before her next several rides. There is no need to lecture her with your handy family policy in place. All you need to say is, "Lia, I see that your helmet is on and you look ready to go to the end of the block and back. Have fun!" Note that this is, of course, just one example. Safety expectations will vary greatly depending on where you live and how much you feel you can trust your child.

Creating family rules together can be a fun process. Once you start, it may be hard to stop. Remember that if there is no real problem with the status quo, creating a rule just to have one is not a meaningful endeavor. Pinpoint your problem areas and keep the focus centered on procedure rather than directly on behavior. Common issues for ground rules at this age include media use, eating habits, bedtime routines, appropriate use of art materials, putting away playthings, and sharing or not sharing certain toys.

Have Heart-to-Heart Discussions

Rules are helpful, but they are not always the answer. Remember that if your child's behavior is worrying you, there may be an underlying issue you need to resolve. When children are hurting inside or are uncomfortable in some way, they often show it by being aggressive, calling others names, withdrawing socially, sneaking behind your back, lying, or flat out refusing to do what you've asked. Before you assume it's time for yet *another* family rule about this particular behavior or attitude, try getting to the root of the problem by having a heart-to-heart discussion.

Find a time when the two of you can be alone in a nonthreatening space. If your child is willing, start by having a cuddle, reading a book, or playing with toys together. As always, open the conversation by acknowledging your child's feelings. For example, "You seemed upset this afternoon when Diego wouldn't share his train set. Are you still feeling sad about that?" Once your child starts to feel comfortable communicating with you, share a relatable story from your own childhood, make suggestions about how to handle a similar situation in the future, and let him know that you are there to help—all he needs to do is come to you and ask. By making time for these heart-to-heart discussions, you are strengthening your relationship and supporting his emotional needs.

Express Gratitude

A child who is enlisted with a special job to do will more likely stay out of mischief and feel empowered by your trust. Involving your child in everyday operations will encourage a cooperative attitude. But keeping little fingers busy is only part of this larger discipline technique. Your child doesn't only want to be your helper; he wants to be appreciated for his efforts as well. And yet when we show our pleasure at his "good" behavior or helpful attitude, we need to be careful not to turn it into empty praise. The profuse use of "good job" or "terrific" when a child is compliant is a behavior modification technique. It rewards, and thus reinforces, certain behaviors and discourages others, but it does not help the child achieve self-discipline, which is what we are after. When we are not around to approve or disapprove, will our children still be respectful of themselves, others, and their environment?

Giving honest, appreciative feedback that bolsters self-esteem and helps self-discipline develop over for the long haul takes some effort on your part. Make it an automatic habit by fully describing the behavior or action you appreciate and then expressing your authentic gratitude for it. You will need to draw the connection between the child's desirable behavior and the outcome. For example, getting ready to leave for preschool has been difficult recently, resulting in tardiness. But this morning, instead of resisting as you urge him out the door, your child has gotten himself dressed and into the car. Before driving away, you take a minute to acknowledge this effort by saying, "I noticed that this morning when I said it was time to get ready to go, you put your shoes on quickly and got in the car right away. You even buckled your own seatbelt. It can be hard to get out the door in the mornings sometimes. Thank you so much for being ready to go. I am looking at the clock and I know we won't be late today. We'll be right on time."

> **Use Your Words:** The next time you are aiming for compliance, try the phrase, "It would be helpful if . . . " For example, "It would be helpful if you keep your blocks on the rug. That way we will be able to see where you are working and won't accidentally step on them."

Spark the Imagination

The art of storytelling opens the doorway to empathy, patience, and inspiration. Our human brains are wired to pay more attention to a good story than a dull, emotionless piece of advice. Since 4-year-olds are learning about storytelling themselves, weaving more complicated themes into their pretend play and describing minor details as well as main points, this is a wonderful time to tap into your own creativity and capture your child's imagination. The more you convey emotion with your tone of voice and use fanciful adjectives to describe ordinary objects, the more captivated your child will be. This technique is particularly useful when your child is whining for that expensive toy at the mall, crabby on a long car ride, or when role-playing a problematic social situation.

Common Issues

The power struggles this year can drag out for ages if you let them. In this section, you'll get a clear plan to circumvent the biggest battles parents face with their 4-year-olds. Your goal is to help your child exit the toddler years with solid self-esteem and a new sense of responsibility.

Fears

Even without outside influence, your 4-year-old may become fixated on dark and scary thoughts, such as the fear of death or of being alone in the dark. Reality and fantasy are indistinguishable, so the concept of a monster eating you up is just as scary and real as the concept of a burglar stealing your possessions. These worries, which may become minor obsessions, are a normal part of your child's development. If they are ignored, your child may reveal his anxiety in nonproductive ways, such as non-compliance, disrupted sleep, or destructive behavior. He needs you to address his fears with reassurance and honesty.

Death

It is a hard reality that sometime in our young lives we must grapple with the concept of our own mortality and that of loved ones. Sometime around age 4, there is a significant moment of awareness. This realization may happen slowly over time or suddenly upon the sight of a dead raccoon in the road, the passing of the family pet, or the loss of a friend or relative. It can be tempting to try to distract your child and urge him toward happier thoughts, or even lie altogether about what happened, but what he needs from you is a serious talk about the life cycles of the living creatures on Earth, including humans.

This is a time for a heart to heart discussion. Listen to his worries and be ready to absorb his grief as he expresses his feelings. Allow him to ask you questions that have unsettling answers such as, "Daddy, will you die?" or "Mommy, why won't the bird fly again?" or even, "Where did Grandpa go when he died?" Sugarcoating these difficult topics with a half-truth or giving fantastical explanations will not satisfy his troubled spirit. Give him the information he needs to know in order to feel secure.

Here are a few truths that your child will appreciate knowing as you have this heart-to-heart discussion:

- All life has a beginning and an end with changes that happen in between. We call this the life cycle.
- Death is part of the life cycle. It is the end.
- Grief is the sadness we feel when we lose someone or something we love.
- It is normal to feel worried about dying and it is normal to grieve when someone or something we love dies.

Reading books about the life cycles of animals or on the topic of grief may help your child to process his emotions. This is also an appropriate time to talk to your child about your personal religious or spiritual beliefs. To avoid confusion, keep the information simplistic and focused. Always end your conversations with calm reassurance that he is loved and safe. Tell him how grateful you are that he is able to ask these big questions and have these deep conversations about life and death.

How Pretend Play Can Help
Sometimes children pretend to be afraid when they are actually not scared at all. By role-playing the part of frightened prey being hunted by a ferocious predator, they are able to safely experience the feeling of "fight or flight." If you get the sense that the fear is truly all an act, feel free to join in playfully and cower under the covers or run away from the imaginary beast. Just be sure to play this game on your child's terms and pause to confirm that all of this is just for pretend. Dramatizing with excessive fantasy can be confusing. That being said, here are a few playful ideas for practicing this emotional state with your child.

The floor is lava: In this game, you put down pillows or small rugs around a designated area and jump from one to another, trying not to touch the "hot lava" with your bare feet. It's also a great way to help them get out their energy indoors, as well as practice their balancing skills.

Animal masks: Sit down and do some crafting with construction paper, scissors, and glue. After making a simple lion or mouse mask, children often enjoy trying them on to assume the different roles. You can demonstrate with brave, powerful movements or skittish, scurrying ones. Take turns and let your child take the lead.

The chase: Whether outside in a big open space or inside a narrow hallway cleared for safety, take turns chasing each other. Most children squeal in delight and giggle when caught. Let your child chase and catch you, too!

Toy props: Don't overlook the pretend play opportunities in a set of dollhouse dolls, puppets, or small barnyard animal toys. When playing with your child, you can give a story-starter with a few of these props and then see how your child fleshes out the plot on his own. For example, "One day, the little mouse was afraid of . . . "

Non-Compliance

A 4-year-old who is physically and emotionally out of control is no fun at all. When he was younger, you could easily scoop him up mid-tantrum and carry him somewhere safer. Not so for a strong and surly older child. The power struggle becomes a parenting paradox: The more you assert your authority and control over your child's actions and demand absolute compliance, the more disobedience you are likely to see. This does not mean that you should allow your child to do whatever he wants, however. A firm yet flexible adult presence is what he needs from you.

Avoiding Power Struggles

You may need to revise your expectations this year for the level of immediate obedience you expect from your child. She is no longer testing boundaries purely for the sake of independent learning. She is also defying you on purpose to test your relationship. As her parent, she trusts you more than anyone else on Earth. Who else gives her such a strong safety net while she makes mistakes, confronts fears, or practices challenging authority?

It may make you uncomfortable when she outright defies you, but think about what this skill will do for her later on in life. Perhaps one day she will stand up to her friends and refuse to participate in bullying another child. As a teen, she may insist on telling an adult when others are engaging in a dangerous activity. Perhaps as an adult she will become active in her local government and stand up for those who are underserved and under-represented in her community. In this context, resisting authority is not a bad skill to have at all.

Address this new skill in a positive way by paying little attention to minor infractions of your family policies. As long as she is being safe and not causing harm to others, it is to your advantage to look the other way. Save the battles for the big stuff.

Overcoming Power Struggles

"You can't make me!" your child boasts. Oh, how tempting it is to reply, "Yes, I can!" Resist engaging in this kind of back and forth. It takes two to argue, and even if you win the battle by using your adult show of force with threats or punishment, your child will likely be so angry or upset and you may feel so exhausted that it will hardly feel like a win at all. If you are clear on exactly why you desire compliance, there are several techniques you can try that will help you follow through, depending on how flexible you can be without compromising safety.

Giving an alternative allows your child to reconsider and take a way out that does not feel humiliating. For example, if your child is running toward the street, stop him physically. Yelling "Stop!" or "Hey!" to get his attention is also appropriate. Then say, "You feel like running. You may not run in the street because it is dangerous. When we get to the park, you will be able to run around all you like. Would you like to hold my hand or walk beside me?" Neither option is likely preferred, but if your child walks a few steps and then breaks impulsively into another run, say, "You chose to run again, so now we will hold hands until it is safe."

Reminding your child of the family policy can work well with a child who tends to be a little bit forgetful. For example, if you find your child eating a snack on the family sofa, you might say, "The rule is that we eat at the table, not on the sofa, because we agreed that we wanted our sofa to stay clean. I expect you to take your dish to the table." This approach offers no flexibility and leaves no room for argument.

Offering some flexibility is okay sometimes, though. If you can give a little, you might get a lot more cooperation in the long run. To allow your child to negotiate, combine the rule with an alternative. This approach would be more like, "The rule is that we eat at the table. Do you feel like today needs to be an exception? If so, I would prefer that you use a tray on your lap so that no food touches the couch. Or perhaps you can sit on the floor picnic-style. What do you think? Would either of those work?" Remember that if you are so flexible that the rules are never enforced, there is no point to them. Breaking a rule now and then is fine, but if you are constantly making exceptions, perhaps you need to re-evaluate the legitimacy of the rule.

Soliciting your child's help is also a great way to gain his cooperation. Most 4-year-olds love to be helpful and feel powerful. For example, if you are running late to your child's yearly checkup with his doctor and he is still barefoot, you might say, "I'm feeling worried that we are going to be late. It would be helpful if you would go grab your shoes. I'm packing our snacks and then we're off! Do you remember where your shoes are?"

Finding the time to sit or lie down together and have a heart-to-heart discussion about his emotions is another way to work to the other side of a power struggle. Any good heart-to-heart talk will naturally include the subject of responsibility and also a reminder of your unconditional love. You really can't say, "I love you," enough to a child.

If your child regularly tries to hook you into a power struggle, he may feel weak and powerless in general. Help him find a way to challenge the status quo for the good of his community. Teach him about age-appropriate environmental concerns, such as littering in his local park and recycling so that ocean creatures do not ingest bits of plastic. Fill his heart with empowering stories of real people in history who fought nonviolently for social justice and made positive changes. Encourage random acts of kindness for both friends and strangers. Talk with him regularly about how good it feels to help others.

Lying

The picture on the wall is crudely drawn, waves of scribbles in bright red. Your child's eyes are wide and her hands clutch something tightly behind her back. You have no doubt it is a crayon. Before you can say more than, "Did you . . . " she blurts, "I didn't do it!" By understanding why your child might choose to lie and learning how to respond in a way that communicates a gentle authority, you will significantly decrease the likelihood of future fibs.

Why Children Lie

Being able to deceive another with words (or at least make the attempt to do so) is a skill that all children must acquire on their way to adulthood. When your child was a baby, she assumed that the objects visually in front of her were the only ones that existed. When an object disappeared from her view, it also disappeared from her awareness. Slowly, over time, she began to understand that objects could be hidden and revealed. You probably played peek-a-boo with her while she was learning the concept. Sometime in toddlerhood, perhaps as early as 2 but certainly by age 6, children learn that one's thoughts can also be hidden and only revealed if one chooses to speak the truth.

Continues on page 134

In-Depth Look:
The Pathway to Peace

A heart-to-heart discussion does not need to be adult-led and spontaneous. Teach your child these steps to resolving any conflict with a focus on inner peace. This method works well for conflicts between siblings or two friends, although it is also useful during adult–child power struggles. It is an excellent alternative to sending your child to a time-out.

1. **Designate a space:** If you are trying to add structure and create a new habit, it helps to have a specific place to do this work. Your peaceful space might be a small table or rug.

2. **Decorate the space:** Place a few beautiful, special décor items that feel pleasant to hold, such as a vase with a faux flower, a paperweight, or a nature item such as a rock or feather. Add a tablecloth if desired, and place a book about peace or friendship in a basket nearby.

3. **Declare the rule:** The person holding the object speaks, and the other person must stay silent and listen.

4. **Practice the process:** Role-play first before using this method during a real conflict. While passing an object back and forth, feelings are expressed from both parties: "I feel _____ because _____" or "I felt _____ when you _____." Then, offer apologies if necessary and make suggestions for solving the problem: "What if we _____ or _____?" When a solution has been agreed upon, celebrate with the phrase, "We have made peace!" Ring a little bell or shake hands to signify this jubilant conclusion.

5. **Mediate:** Until everyone fully understands how to express feelings and take turns, adult intervention is essential. Sometimes children (especially the very young or those with social-emotional differences) are not comfortable expressing their feelings, so you may speak on their behalf and assist with offering possible solutions.

6. **Meditate:** Go to this peaceful space alone. Hold an object in your hand and breathe slowly and rhythmically. Say a prayer or recite a short poem. Tell your child that you are practicing finding inner peace. This space can also be used as a place to calm down when hyper, or to unwind after a stimulating day.

Cultivating a mindful, peaceful attitude will empower your child to address her strong emotions nonviolently in any future conflicts.

Continued from page 131

Because children younger than 6 do not distinguish between fantasy and reality very well, a child may even believe her own lie as she speaks it. For a young child, the act of lying is not the same as it is for adults at all. It is a sign that your child is invoking her imagination to change her reality, no different than when she plays pretend. While she is growling like a lion, she imagines her claws flexing with power, sees herself chasing hyenas, and feels strong and brave. And when she insists that she did not draw on the wall, she is wishing with all her might that it were true.

How to Handle a Lie

Lying is a developmental milestone you can inwardly celebrate, even if you outwardly express disapproval. Many parents have the mistaken impression that lying indicates disrespect for authority. Punishing a child for wrongdoing and then again for lying about it will unfortunately have the opposite effect the parent intends. The fear of punishment will exacerbate the lying problem, not eliminate it. The way to stop a child from lying is by ignoring the lie at first to focus on the reason for the lying, which is the fear of being caught.

First, if at all possible, don't give her the opportunity to lie. By asking if she drew on the wall when you already know the truth, you are setting her up. Call it like you see it right away. For example, say, "There is a crayon drawing on the wall," or, "You drew on the wall." Many children will choose to confess at this point. If she does lie, however, remember that she also wishes that she had not done it; even though she was caught red-handed, she is still somewhat naive. Scribbling on the wall might have been an impulsive act, or it may have been a way to get your attention. It is possible that something has been troubling her emotionally.

Your next step is to get to the root of the underlying problem before you address the lie. If cleanup is needed, as in the case of the crayon on the wall, give her information first. "Paper is for drawing. Crayon can damage the paint on the walls." Encourage her to help clean up the mess. Rather than demanding, offer to do it together.

While you work on cleaning up or after you are finished, have a heart-to-heart discussion. She needs to know that when she does something wrong, she doesn't need to lie to you about it. You might ask, "Were you worried that I would be mad? What did you think would happen when I found out?" Empathize by telling her a brief story about a time when you did something wrong and didn't want anyone to find out. Talk about the concept of *guilt* and how it is our brain's way of letting us know we may have made a mistake. Explain how lies interfere with the trust two people have for each other.

Collaborate on a plan for the future. What might she do next time she feels she has made a mistake? How might you react? When you address lies using this method, your child will learn that lying is not necessary or desirable—in fact, admitting a mistake is immensely more comforting because she feels loved unconditionally.

Gray Areas

Consider whether you are modeling honesty in daily life. If you lie to your child, you need to expect that he will return the favor. Sooner or later, you will also need to discuss the subjects of white lies, tall tales, and half-truths. How appropriate these are for use in different social situations will vary depending on your cultural values. If a white lie is acceptable in your culture, try to put a finger on exactly when and why. Your child will most certainly be aware of these lies and may be confused. Address these issues as they come up naturally in life, such as when you thank someone for an unwanted gift.

Social Relationships

Enthusiasm for exploring social relationships is a running theme for 4-year-olds. The work your child does in the social-emotional department is extremely important for developing a healthy self-image. Your goal is to help your child navigate conflicts with peers in order to foster healthy friendships. By playing with a variety of children who have different physical characteristics, personalities, skill levels, and cultural values, your child will learn to respect the striking similarities and differences among humans. These experiences are setting the stage for all future interactions.

Defining Friendships

How our hearts ache for the child who angrily or sadly reveals that a former best friend "won't let me play with her," or the surprising reverse announcement of "She's not my friend. I don't like her anymore." Before we get too uptight or defensive on her behalf, we need to put the entire concept of 4-year-old friendships into perspective. Your child may get along more easily with some children than others, but her idea of being a good friend is different from yours or even a 10-year-old's. In her eyes, friends, even "girlfriends" or "boyfriends," are just other children who play with her and nothing more.

Parent to Parent:
A New Perspective on Lying

"I don't remember the very first lie my son told me, but as soon as he turned 4, he started lying constantly. I was going crazy until I realized it was a linguistic and cognitive development. We had a talk about this fun new skill he had, and how it showed me his brain was growing. I also had to explain the difference between a 'white' lie and a lie that can really hurt someone. Some untruths are acceptable when we use them to keep a surprise party or a proposal a secret, but they aren't acceptable when they can potentially harm people. I also made sure that telling the truth didn't get him in trouble even if the offense would normally be followed with some consequence. The perpetual lying calmed down within a few months."

— *Rachel, 35, from Nashville,*
Tennessee, parent of two children
(ages 4 years and 11 months)

Her interpretation of social interactions cannot be trusted wholly. She just isn't a reliable source of information. When that friend unexpectedly wants to play with another child one day or decides to play a different game instead of the one your child enjoys most, the rejection can feel intensely unfair—even devastating. A heart-to-heart discussion is almost always called for in this case, as is help with expressing those feelings and resolving the conflict with the friend. Using the "pathway to peace" method (page 132) is effective here.

> **Quick Tip:** This is the age when many children take a social interest in exploring body parts, playing "doctor," and perhaps even touching their genitals in public. It is perfectly normal for children to be curious. Children should never be made to feel ashamed of their bodies. However, you must teach them what behavior is appropriate in public and what personal activities are best handled in private. The topic of consent is also an important one to address: No one has the right to touch your body without permission.

Group Dynamics

Group play exclusions are equally common at this age, although they can be quickly stopped. The social interactions of 4-year-olds do not need to be micromanaged, but they definitely require adult supervision and reminders. A sing-songy rule can help, as children will often remind their peers of the rules if they notice infractions.

A helpful example of this would be the phrase, "You can't say 'you can't play,'" meaning that the exclusion of others is not allowed. The child who was excluded may also need help knowing how to join. If everyone in the sandbox has already chosen a role to play, she may not know what to do. You can help her by making observations about what you notice and suggestions for a role she may enjoy.

Rude Behavior
While 4-year-olds can be sweet and lovey-dovey, they can also be rude and crabby, even when they don't mean it. At this age, your child's expressive language capabilities have taken an enormous leap. He's learning so many verbal arts, from using appropriately descriptive adjectives to name-calling and attacking with words. Much of this practice, however rude it seems, is still innocent. Your child might not yet know that calling an overweight person fat is hurtful and insensitive, or that blurting out "I hate you!" or "You're stupid!" is not a nice way to treat someone who cares for you. When your child uses words inappropriately in public, it can be a humiliating experience for everyone.

Since many of these statements are made for the sake of getting your attention, it may be in your best interest to ignore some of them in the heat of the moment, especially the name-calling. If, however, you feel that it is a matter of a lack of information, your child will benefit greatly from your instruction. Use a picture book to point out the physical differences of one of the characters. Ask your child to imagine how that person might feel if she were called a rude name or spoken to in a mean way because of her differences. You cannot teach a child empathy directly, but you can nudge him in the right direction. Depending on your child's temperament, he may need more direct instruction about how to engage appropriately in a variety of social settings. But with your guidance, he will learn.

Quick Tip: Your child will be listening to the language you use when you're frustrated. If you or other adults or children regularly use swear words around your child, expect to hear them crop up in your child's language. In fact, if you are using swear words yourself, it is unreasonable to expect your child not to mimic you. If you ban the swear words, you are more or less asking for a power struggle. It's much more developmentally appropriate at this age to acknowledge that words have power and that some words are considered rude. Modeling alternative phrasing gives them something else to say that expresses the same feeling or sentiment. Example: Instead of "damn it," you can model the lesser expletives, "Oops!" or "Whoopsadoodle!" You also make an effort to express your feelings in more positive ways, such as "I'm so frustrated!" And after this, you should ignore your child's use of them as much as possible. Paying attention to these words will no doubt increase their use.

Whining

Pleading and needling, begging and nagging—even the words that define the act of whining sound, well, *whiny*. And those drawling syllables get more annoying the longer they go on. Children of all ages whine, and it won't go away just because you ask your child to "say it in a regular voice." In fact, if you really want to hear a lot more whining, the best way to encourage it is to mimic the whine and complain about how annoying it is just before you give in and allow him to have or do whatever he was whining about. Giving in reinforces this behavior.

Why Children Whine

The truth is that you have the power to teach your child more appropriate ways of getting your attention. When he's whining, he might not even be aware that he's doing it. The time for this lesson, however, is not while your child is whining. Pick a different time, preferably when your child is well-rested and happy to role-play with you. During the actual whining, as irritating as it is, you must ignore the attention-getting method. What you want to focus on is the real reason for the whine, which is most likely not specifically the candy bar at the checkout line. You'll have to look deeper.

Children tend to whine when they are bored, frustrated, hungry, tired, or feeling ignored. When we are concentrating on other things, such as while driving or grocery shopping, it can be easy to miss the little signals that our children are getting worked up. Even if we do notice them, we may be feeling so rushed and frazzled that we ignore them completely, making a whine even more likely.

Putting an End to the Whining

When your child whines, the first thing to do is steel your resolve. It is easy to cave in to just about anything when you just want the irritating noise to cease. But if you really want to stop the whining, you need to stop what you're doing and give your child your full attention. If you do not, the situation is likely to escalate. Get down on her level and give her eye contact if possible. Physical contact, such as putting your hands on her shoulders or holding her hands in yours is also effective if she consents. Empathize with her feelings. For example, you might say, "I hear your voice and you sound frustrated. It can be hard to shop when you're tired and you just want to go home."

Many children will breathe a sigh of relief when their emotions have been acknowledged and they feel understood. Others will persist in the whining. Let your child know that you are setting a limit and will not fulfill the request. Do your absolute best to ignore the behavior, but do show that you care. Sometimes a snack will help distract her. Indulging in a fantasy is also a fun and effective way to change everyone's mood. For example, if she's moaning and groaning about how long it takes to get home, say, "I agree. This car ride is so booooring. Next time I'm buying a car with wings. Then I'd push a button, the wings would spread out from underneath, and we would just fly straight home, right over all of these stoplights!" When you pull out a humorous trick like this, most 4-year-olds will forget all about whining, eager to join you in the game. It works for about just about everything. If she's complaining about wanting to stop for ice cream, state your limit first and then invite your child into the fantasy: "I'm not stopping for ice cream, but I sure wish I was! I'd order the mintiest chocolate chip they have. What flavor would you choose?"

While she may continue to use a whiny voice now and then over the next several years, if you respond with obvious compassion and a touch of humor *without giving in* she will learn other ways to communicate her needs.

Use Your Words: Many children will continue to ask repeatedly when you have already given them an answer. This is a sign that your child is lacking confidence and asking for support. A phrase you may find helpful is, "I have already answered that question. Do you remember what I said?" If your child cannot repeat it back to you, this is a sign that you were not clear enough the first time. If he does summarize your previous answer, you might follow it with the phrase, "It sounds like you know what to do! Is there anything else I can do for you?"

Resources and Reference

Resources

Support for parents abounds if you know where to look. There are many excellent sources of information on child development and gentle discipline techniques. I have listed a few of my favorites here to help you navigate any specific areas of concern you may be facing with your toddler.

- Centers for Disease Control and Prevention (CDC), https:// www.cdc.gov/parents/: Articles and recommendations from the CDC as applied to child development and parenting with reference to developmental milestones.

- *Discipline for Life: Getting it Right with Children* by Madelyn Swift: A positive yet no-nonsense approach to discipline with frequent reminders of the most important life lessons.

- *The Emotional Life of the Toddler* by Alicia F. Lieberman: An in-depth examination of toddlers' emotional development with plenty of good insight for parents.

- *The No-Cry Sleep Solution for Toddlers and Preschoolers* by Elizabeth Pantley: Solving typical sleep issues and bedtime struggles during early childhood.

- *No Drama Discipline* by Daniel J. Siegel, M.D. and Tina Payne Bryson, PhD: Information about the cognitive abilities and limitations of young children as they relate to discipline strategies.

- *Oh Crap! Potty Training* by Jamie Glowacki: Solid information and practical advice for introducing the toilet and addressing regressions.

- *Peaceful Parent, Happy Kids* by Dr. Laura Markham: How to stop yelling by connecting with your children and regulating your own emotions.

- *Positive Discipline: The First Three Years* by Jane Nelsen, Ed.D., Cheryl Erwin, M.A., and Roslyn Ann Duffy: Common behaviors of children from birth to age 3 with suggested positive discipline strategies for parents.

- *Positive Discipline for Preschoolers* by Jane Nelsen, Ed.D., Cheryl Erwin, M.A., and Roslyn Ann Duffy: Common behaviors of children ages 3 to 5 with suggested positive discipline strategies for parents.

- *Unconditional Parenting* by Alfie Kohn: Using a love-based, unconditional approach to parenting without rewards or punishments.

- *Your One-Year-Old: Fun-loving and Fussy* by Louise Bates Ames, PhD: Developmental insight for parents of 1-year-old children.

- *Your Two-Year-Old: Terrible or Tender* by Louise Bates Ames, PhD: The mysteries of typical 2-year-olds unveiled.

- *Your Three-Year-Old: Friend or Enemy* by Louise Bates Ames, PhD: All of the ins and outs of what it means to be an average 3-year-old.

- *Your Four-Year-Old: Wild and Wonderful* by Louise Bates Ames, PhD: An explanation of 4-year-old behavior and characteristics of this age.

Reference

Thomas, Alexander, Stella Chess, and Herbert G. Birch. "The origin of personality." *Scientific American* 223, no. 2 (1970): 102–109. http://acamedia.info/sciences/sciliterature/origin_of_personality.htm

Index

Acknowledgments

Henry and Jude, I love you madly. When you were little, raising you was never easy. As you grew, pushing boundaries to assert your independence, I had so many mama worries. I cried with you when you grieved. I cheered with you when you felt brave and successful. Sometimes I lost my temper, too. I'm not proud of the times when I lacked patience, but I'm a better person because of you. Without feeling the full intensity of your toddler tantrums, I never could have written the words in this book.

David, I can't imagine parenting without your calm, sympathetic presence. In the middle of managing tantrums and acts of defiance, you kept me grounded by reminding me what our children might be feeling and asking again and again how we could work together to meet their emotional needs. You are my partner and my soulmate; thank you for your guidance and encouragement.

Kate, Amy, Kari, Gayle, and Rachel—your willingness to share your parenting experiences is much appreciated. Thank you for your wisdom and kindness.

Thank you to everyone who supported me along this journey: my parents, my mama friends near and far, the Montessori community, Breana Sylvester, my editor Katie Moore, and the Callisto Media team. Many generous and talented hands have touched every page.

About the Author

Aubrey Hargis, MEd, is a parent coach and educational consultant best known for her empathetic approach and appreciation for the magic of childhood. She is the author of *Baby's First Year Milestones: Promote and Celebrate Your Baby's Development with Monthly Games and Activities.* As the founder of the Child Development Institute of the Redwoods, she creates online courses and coaches parents in compassionate discipline techniques and Montessori education. Aubrey lives with her husband and two children under a blanket of San Francisco fog, where the coastal cliffs and nearby redwood trails are always beckoning for another adventure. Visit her online at ChildoftheRedwoods.com.

CPSIA information can be obtained
at www.ICGtesting.com
Printed in the USA
LVHW051000040319
609389LV00015B/385/P